A MODERN HISTORY OF THE JEWS

FROM THE MIDDLE AGES TO THE PRESENT DAY

A MODERN HISTORY OF THE JEWS

FROM THE MIDDLE AGES TO THE PRESENT DAY

Tells the story of Judaism from the medieval ghettos through the Enlightenment to the tragedy of the Holocaust and the birth of modern Israel, with over 250 illustrations

Lawrence Joffe

southwater

This edition is published by Southwater,
an imprint of Anness Publishing Ltd,
108 Great Russell Street,
London WC1B 3NA;
info@anness.com

www.southwaterbooks.com; www.annesspublishing.com; twitter: @Anness_Books

Anness Publishing has a new picture agency outlet for images for publishing, promotions or advertising. Please visit our website www.practicalpictures.com for more information.

A CIP catalogue record for this book is available from the British Library.

Publisher: Joanna Lorenz
Senior Editor: Felicity Forster
Maps: Peter Bull Art Studio
Designer: Nigel Partridge
Production Controller: Pirong Wang

Previously published as part of a larger volume,
An Illustrated History of the Jewish People

Page 1 *Kiddush cup.*
Page 2 *Orthodox Jews in New York during Rosh Hashanah.*
Page 3 *Moroccan Jews at a celebration honouring the medieval philosopher Maimonides.*

Above *A klezmer band at a welcoming party, c.1920.*

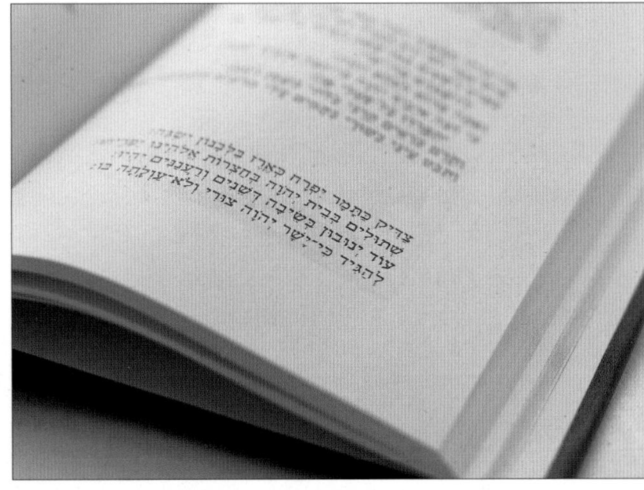

Above *A book of Shabbat blessings.*

CONTENTS

Above Gravestones destroyed by Nazis in memorial wall, Krakow.

Introduction

In 1492 Spain expelled the world's most cultured Jewish community, yet what seemed like a final death knell for Jews everywhere merely proved an interlude.

The tale of Jewish survival is full of extraordinary drama – triumph followed by setbacks, and miraculous rebirths following periods of near extinction. Such changes in fortune have persisted to modern times.

As Jews have established communities throughout the world, other cultures have enriched the Jewish story and identity. In return, individual Jews have made a profound impact on civilization, from Moses and Jesus Christ to Maimonides and Albert Einstein.

MIDDLE EASTERN ROOTS

In a sense, the Jewish narrative has recently returned to where it began, the Middle East, and in particular a small pivotal area along the eastern Mediterranean known as the Land of Israel to Jews, and historical Palestine to others.

Below Built in 1763, the Touro Synagogue in Newport, Rhode Island, is the USA's oldest still operating today.

ENDURANCE

Jewish communities have always experienced one common condition: a fascinating tension between a core Jewish identity and a need or desire to adapt to surrounding cultures. Jews in turn have enriched their host societies.

Christianity sprang from Judaism in the 1st century, and Jewish beliefs also influenced Islam, which arose in the 7th century. Adherents of Judaism's two 'sister faiths' currently number more than 3.5 billion people, vastly outnumbering today's 14 million Jews. Nonetheless, Judaism has endured, partly thanks to the compendium of writing called the Talmud, which united Jews in their particular belief traditions.

Above Jerusalem's Dome of the Rock is a sacred site for both Jews and Muslims.

Running parallel to this history is the reality of anti-Semitism, a virulent and ever-evolving hatred of Jews and their beliefs. For instance, the 'Golden Age' of Spain, a period of unprecedented creativity and interfaith cooperation, ended when Christian leaders saw Jews as a threat and expelled them in 1492. Similar patterns were repeated elsewhere in Europe.

NEW HORIZONS

This book picks up the experience of those Jews who fled Spain and found a haven within the Muslim Ottoman Empire, in North Africa, Anatolia, the Balkans and much of the Middle East. A few landed in eastern Europe, which increasingly became a new hub.

During the Enlightenment and Emancipation periods, Jews emerged from the physical and notional ghettos that had cordoned them off from the rest of society. Confronted by modernity, many experienced a crisis of faith which sharpened divisions between traditionalists and reformists. Some joined schismatic, revivalist or messianic sects; others abandoned Jewish life altogether.

An extraordinary 19th-century Ashkenazi demographic boom coincided with persecution in the Russian empire, where most Jews then resided. Such factors drove mass migration from Europe to America, which increasingly became a new fulcrum of Jewish life. Within decades, Jews who once spoke Yiddish or Ladino now thought, wrote and conversed in English; former pedlars saw their children enter academia and the professions.

TRANSFORMATIONS

New ideologies proliferated, too, including liberalism, socialism, ethnic nationalism and Zionism – a movement to reclaim the 'promised land'. Then came the catastrophe of the Nazis' World War II Holocaust, which murdered six million Jews and almost destroyed two millennia of their presence in Europe.

Miraculously, the Jewish people saw Israel's birth in 1948 and its development, if troubled and often criticized, as a new axis of Jewish identity. Hebrew, once confined to synagogue liturgy, became a living language once more.

The story that becomes apparent is one of survival despite adversity, dreadful miscalculations and remarkable innovations; of a tenacious population of thriving communities from Argentina to Singapore; and of individuals who have made inspiring contributions to the arts, sciences, academia, the global economy and world culture generally.

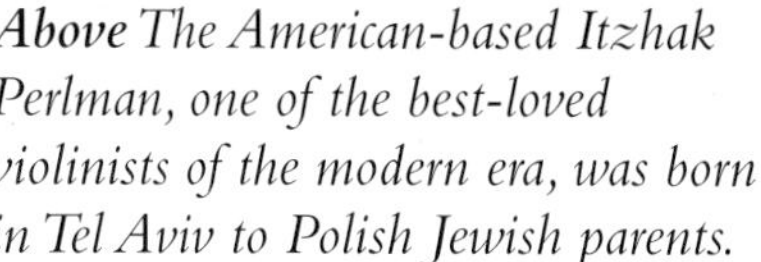

***Above** The American-based Itzhak Perlman, one of the best-loved violinists of the modern era, was born in Tel Aviv to Polish Jewish parents.*

IN THIS BOOK

This volume outlines the many post-15th century developments that led Jews, both individually and as a group, to enrich modern society. It is divided into six chapters, covering the Jewish revival east and west; a changing faith; revolution and emancipation; World Wars and the Holocaust; Zionism, Jerusalem and Israel; and Jewish culture in modern society. What emerges is not so much one history as a series of histories across continents, linked by a common thread of shared identity. Jews still defy easy categorization as primarily a race, a religion or a nation. Yet their experience of migration and resettlement, both voluntary and enforced, is shared by millions across the world today, providing a model for other peoples to draw on. Maps, evocative photography and instructive text bring the narrative to life, telling one of the world's most devastating, but exciting, stories of human survival.

***Below** Jews who resisted Nazis in the Warsaw Ghetto Uprising being rounded up by the SS in 1943.*

CHAPTER 1

JEWISH REVIVAL EAST AND WEST

For Jews everywhere, the Spanish expulsions of 1492 seemed to snuff out a light that would never be relit. In fact, the calamity coincided with several new opportunities. That same year Columbus sailed to the 'New World', opening up previously unimagined prospects for traders. Printing technology disseminated knowledge more easily than ever before. And the Ottomans allowed Spanish exiles to settle across their empire, including Palestine.

Within two centuries, Dutch Sephardim became the first Jews to return to England, and Amsterdam produced Baruch Spinoza, arguably the greatest of early Jewish freethinkers. Yet Italy invented the ghetto, and a German reformist Christian movement known as Protestantism turned from sympathizing with Jews to deriding them. Overall, the period from 1492 saw a gradual passing of the torch from Sephardi to Ashkenazi culture, as Poland grew in stature as a Jewish centre, Yiddish flourished as a language and Rabbi Loew spearheaded a Jewish Renaissance in Prague.

***Opposite** The Dutch master Rembrandt (1609–69) often painted Jewish subjects, such as this striking portrait of a rabbi. Amsterdam became home to Jews, both Ashkenazi and Sephardi.*

***Above** Bridge to the Jewish ghetto in Venice. A sudden influx of Spanish Jewish refugees led to the founding of the first established ghetto in the world in March 1516.*

Jews in New Cultures

The late 15th century saw Jews evicted from Spain and Portugal, Naples and Nuremberg. Yet fresh communities sprouted in Poland, the Netherlands, Persia, and even the Americas.

Jews survived despite the expulsions and persecution of the turbulent 16th century. They created new institutions, harnessed new technology and kept alive old traditions of scholarship. Jews thrived by creating intricate trading networks that linked their new places of refuge – Ottoman Turkey, North Africa, the Netherlands, Poland and Lithuania.

NEW HAVENS

Paradoxically, the expulsions put Sephardi and Ashkenazi Jews in contact with each other to their mutual advantage. This was especially true of the Netherlands and, later, north-west Germany, areas that came under Protestant rule and accepted 'New Christians' (converted Jews) from Spain and Portugal. As a result of this, Jews repopulated the shores of the Atlantic after years of absence, just as the Atlantic began to take over from the Mediterranean as the prime focus of European trade.

Iberian (Sephardi) Jews also flocked to the Ottoman empire, while most German Ashkenazim moved *en masse* to Poland. Thus Sephardi–Ashkenazi co-operation grew as Poland became the chief transit for expanding overland trade between the Ottomans and central and western Europe.

Below Established in 1516, the Venice Ghetto set a pattern for similar enclaves for Jews across Europe.

THE GHETTOS

In March 1516, panicked by a sudden influx of Spanish Jewish refugees, Venice set up the world's first ghetto, so called because the area was an old iron foundry (*ghetto* in Italian). Most of the original inhabitants were of German origin; Jews from the Levant got their own ghetto in 1541. Other Italian cities set up ghettos: Rome in 1556, Florence in 1571, Verona in 1605, Mantua in 1612 and Ferrara in 1624.

The word ghetto has come to signify an area of urban depravity, but there were positive aspects: during nightly curfews Jews were protected from bigots outside the walls; during daylight hours they still traded in the city. They alone were allowed to pursue loan-banking, a trade which, although it never yielded vast fortunes, spread prosperity throughout some 300 Italian communities during the period 1300–1500. Isolated from gentile society, these Jews nurtured a distinctive culture within the ghetto.

Above A beautiful ketubah, *Jewish marriage contract, from Modena, Italy, 1723, with a view of Jerusalem.*

FALSE HOPE IN PORTUGAL

By the 13th century Portugal's Jews numbered 200,000, a fifth of the total population; and King João II valued his Jewish financiers and gun-makers for most of his 1481–94 reign. After some 150,000 refugees poured across the border from Spain in 1492, however, João declared non-domiciled Jews to be slaves, and ordered that Jewish children should be separated from their parents. João's successor, Manuel, reversed these decrees, only to order all Jews to leave Portugal in October 1497. Three thousand Iberian crypto-Jews died in a pogrom in Lisbon in 1506.

In 1531 Pope Clement VII (1478–1534) began a Portuguese Inquisition aimed at 'secretly Jewish' Maranos: several thousand were imprisoned and many more fled.

SICILY, MALTA AND ITALY

The Spanish expulsions and the period leading up to them affected Jews well beyond the Spanish mainland. In 1391 some 300 were murdered by mobs in Majorca. After 1492, Jews were forced out of Spanish-ruled Sicily and southern Italy. Most constructed new secure lives in Ottoman territory.

Pope Alexander VI (1431–1503) allowed Jews from Sicily, Sardinia and Spain to settle in his Italian states. Many fled to papal Naples, but after it fell to Spain, Jews were evicted in 1510 and 'new Christians' (converted Jews) in 1515. As late as 1587, the duchy of Milan banished 900 Jews when it, too, came under Spanish rule. Nor were all popes so benign: in 1556 Paul IV (1478–1559) sent 24 Portuguese Maranos to burn at the stake in Ancona.

THE NEW WORLD

In 1502, on his final visit to the New World, Christopher Columbus left behind 52 Jewish-origin families in Costa Rica.

The Spanish and Portuguese began to hunt down insincere converts in their New World colonies. As early as 1515 the authorities deported one 'secret Jew' from Hispaniola (now Cuba) to face the Inquisition in Spain. Maranos were offered the choice of death or 'true conversion' at autos-da-fé in Lima, Peru (1570), Mexico City (1574), Cartagena, Colombia (1610) and Havana.

By 1640, Jews and Maranos were living safely along the Brazilian coast under Dutch rule. One town, Bahia, was even nicknamed 'The Rock of Israel'. After Portugal reconquered Brazil in 1654, resident Jews fled to nearby Surinam and Cayenne and to the Caribbean. Twenty-three Brazilian Sephardim arrived in Dutch-ruled New Amsterdam (later called New York), where they established She'arit Israel, the first Hebrew congregation in North America.

PERSIA

Meanwhile, Jews thousands of miles to the east suffered too. In 1511 the usually downtrodden Shia sect took over Persia and established its first empire since the Fatimids ruled Egypt. Their clerics forced Persia's new Safavid rulers to discriminate against Jews and Christians.

Above Lorenzo de Medici (1449–92), ruler of Florence, who protected his Jewish subjects from expulsions.

Respite came when the urbane Abbas I (1588–1629) invited Jews to settle in his new capital, Isfahan, in 1592. They welcomed his peace treaty with the rival Ottoman Caliphate and his expansion of seafaring trade with Europe, in which they played a pivotal role.

Next, Shah Abbas II of Persia (r. 1642–66) drove Jews from Isfahan in 1652 on grounds of 'ritual impurity', and forced 100,000 Jews to adopt Islam. Confronted by a Jewish delegation in 1661, Abbas relented and allowed Jews to revert to their old faith, as long as they wore a distinctive patch.

Life improved for Jews in 1736 when invasions by Sunni Muslim Afghans destroyed the Safavid dynasty. Many became physicians, pharmacists and international merchants. However, they never reached the intellectual heights of their co-religionists in a Europe where the Renaissance promised new hope.

Left The current building for Congregation She'arit Israel, New York City, for a community established in 1654.

INTELLECTUAL STIRRINGS

DURING THE RENAISSANCE AND THE REFORMATION, JEWS REMAINED THE ONLY RELIGIOUS MINORITY WITHIN CHRISTENDOM. THE ADVENT OF PRINTING LED TO INCREASING INTEREST IN HEBREW TEXTS.

Europe of the 15th, 16th and 17th centuries was a ferment of change. The Italian Renaissance encouraged artistic individualism, rational inquiry and renewed interest in long-neglected classics. Protestants in Germany and France challenged the 1,200-year-long dominance of the Roman Catholic Church and were soon to split the continent apart. Other truth-seekers rejected Christianity altogether.

Meanwhile, scientific breakthroughs allowed for voyages of discovery and helped create Europe's first overseas empires. In time the new mercantile class began seeking greater domestic freedoms. Europeans often oppressed the peoples of Africa, Asia and the Americas, however, and colonial rivalries led to bloody wars abroad and at home. In addition, developing colonies demanded slaves, which led to a trade in human cargo that shamed their liberal and Christian values.

Below Solomon and the Queen of Sheba, *c.1555, by Tintoretto, an Italian Renaissance artist fascinated by Jewish and biblical themes.*

EUROPE'S SOLE MINORITY

Throughout this period Jews remained the only religious minority within Christendom. The changes around them had decidedly mixed effects on their community, for while attacks on Church authority created space for free expression, challenges to religion threatened their faith as well. Anti-Semitism refused to disappear despite the spirit of liberalism.

Jews who initially welcomed Protestantism, for instance, were shocked when Martin Luther took to Jew-baiting. Even the great Dutch humanist Desiderius Erasmus of Rotterdam wrote: 'If it is the part of a good Christian to detest the Jews, then we are all good Christians'.

ב עזר אלהי קדם שוכן
מעונה : אחל לפרש
תפלות כל השנה ::

Above *The first book printed in Lisbon, the* Book of Abraham, *published in Hebrew by Eliezer Toledano, 1489.*

PRINTING REVOLUTION

One escape from isolation came via printing, which democratized knowledge and defied borders. After Johann Gutenberg made the world's first Bible with movable type in 1445, Jews produced at least 180 Hebrew printed titles between 1472 and 1500. Most were religious works.

The first printing press of any language in the Orient was a Jewish firm, which printed Hebrew books in Constantinople in 1493. Italy became the centre for Hebrew printing, although many master printers were German Jews. The Jewish Soncino family, for instance, originally hailed from Bavaria and settled near Milan. They also printed in Brescia, Rimini, Pesaro, Constantinople and Salonika.

Perhaps the most accomplished craftsman of all was Daniel Bomberg, a Christian from Belgium, primarily active in Venice between 1516 and 1549. He printed the entire multi-volume Talmud between 1520 and 1523 in Venice and set the pagination standards for Talmuds for all time. The technical advance of printing spread Jewish knowledge like wildfire.

Left *Galileo explaining his daring scientific insights at Padua University; from a painting of 1873, Mexico.*

OFFICIAL CENSORSHIP

Catholic governors were worried about dissident literature being spread, so they introduced tight censorship and ordered Talmuds and other Jewish books burned in 1554. Production resumed 11 years later, but only once copies were vetted to rid them of negative references to Jesus or gentiles.

Censorship was not unknown to Jews. Conservative French rabbis persuaded Dominicans to burn copies of Maimonides' 'Guide' in Montpellier, France, in 1233. Nine years later they watched as thousands of Talmuds were set ablaze in Paris by papal order, aware that they had precipitated this self-inflicted tragedy.

Below: Jewish Kabbalist holding a 'tree of life' diagram of divine attributes; from a book of magic, Portae Lucis, *1516.*

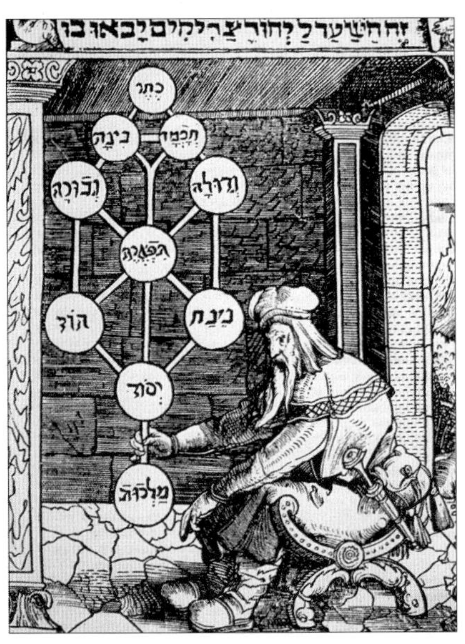

THE RENAISSANCE

A 15th-century revival of interest in Greek and Latin classics soon spawned curiosity in texts in Hebrew, which Italian and later German scholars came to regard as the third of the great 'classical literatures'. For Jews, literature, music and the sciences presented better chances for creative expression. One Jewish pioneer was the court composer Salomone di Rossi, who wrote European-style melodies for the ancient synagogue liturgy.

FREE THINKERS

The Renaissance encouraged Italian Jews to broach taboos and to discuss ideas with gentile interlocutors. Azaria di Rossi, for instance, revisited contentious issues of belief first raised by the 1st-century Egyptian Jewish philosopher Philo. Leone Modena taught Christians about Jewish practices and did much to demystify Jews in the public eye.

One of the most daring Jewish thinkers was Solomon Ibn Verga (*c.*1450–*c.*1525). He wrote *The Rod of Judah*, sometimes called the first secularist Jewish history since Josephus. A dedicated rationalist, Ibn Verga criticized the Talmud and mocked Maimonides, chided Jews for being 'twice naked' by neglecting political and military science, and blamed anti-Semitism on Jews who 'show themselves lords and masters, therefore the masses envy them'.

The Renaissance spirit also took hold in Holland under Calvinist Protestant rule, where the established *ma'amad*, or 'executive body of the Sephardi community', had no truck for dissent. Uriel da Costa set an example to other Jewish freethinkers. Born in 1585 in Oporto, Portugal, and raised as a Jesuit, he reconverted to Judaism and fled from persecution to Holland. He questioned the Oral Law and wrote scathingly about the ritualistic 'Pharisees of Amsterdam', who excommunicated him. Da Costa rejoined the community in 1640, but killed himself after being forced to receive 39 lashes in the synagogue by way of 'recantation'.

Below *An anti-Semitic pamphlet from Frankfurt, 1601, shows a ritual murder and Jews suckling a pig.*

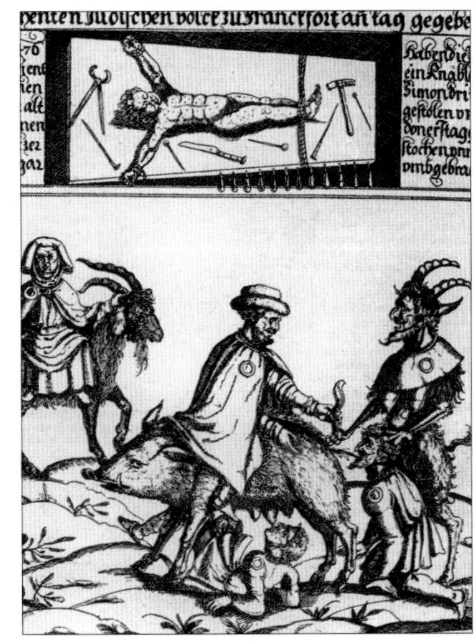

Jewish Communities in Germany

By the 16th century, the Holy Roman empire seemed like a throwback to medieval times, when religion and monarchical dynasties, not nationality, defined Europe.

Germany was not a distinct state until the mid-19th century. Before that, the Holy Roman empire encompassed most of what is today Germany, as well as Switzerland, Austria, Slovenia, Belgium, Luxembourg, the Czech Republic and Holland, plus parts of France, Poland and northern Italy. Far from being a truly united entity, the empire comprised hundreds of smaller kingdoms, principalities, counties and free imperial cities.

EASTERN EXTREMITIES

From a Jewish perspective, greater Germany was particularly uninviting in the 15th century: Jews were expelled from Vienna, Linz, Cologne, Augsburg, Bavaria and Styria, southern Austria, in 1496. Increasingly Jews moved eastwards, through the empire's extremities to Moravia, Bohemia and on to Poland.

Below *Built in 1175, this synagogue in Worms, sometimes called Rashi's Chapel, is the oldest in Germany.*

Right *Martin Luther, the dynamo behind the Protestant Revolution, at first inspired hope in Jews. Danish altarpiece, 1561.*

Jewish fortunes revived by the late 16th century: the Emperor Maximilian II (r. 1557–76) allowed Jews to return to towns in Bohemia, and in 1577 his son, Rudolph II, gave them a charter of privileges. Poland, meanwhile, emerged as the new Ashkenazi heartland; some Jews made fortunes there and further east, effectively running vast Ukrainian and Lithuanian estates that provided grain to expanding western Europe.

THE PFEFFERKORN AFFAIR

Jews discovered friends in unexpected places, such as Johannes Reuchlin, a German Christian humanist and Hebrew scholar inspired by the winds of change emanating from Italy. In 1509 Johannes Pfefferkorn, a Jewish-born Dominican monk in Cologne, declared: 'Whoever afflicts the Jews is doing the will of God'. He sought to kidnap Jewish children and raise them as Catholics. He also won imperial approval to confiscate all Jewish books, especially the Talmud. Soon Jewish tomes were set alight in Frankfurt; while 38 Jews were burned in Berlin on trumped-up charges of child murder. Reuchlin argued for the Jews, forcing the emperor to rescind his edict in 1510. The controversy raged for years.

THE REFORMATION

For more than a millennium, Roman Catholicism reigned in most of Europe. As the Byzantine empire drew to a close in 1453, Greek or Christian Orthodox pockets in western Europe, such as Ravenna in Adriatic Italy, died out. The Church of Rome isolated and eliminated competing trends, like Gnosticism and Arianism in the 3rd century, the Cathars in the 14th and Hussites in the 15th. All were called heresies, and several movements were ostracized precisely because they seemed to be too close to Judaism.

With the pope at its head the Catholic Church seemed impregnable. However, a string of corrupt popes weakened it, and resentments came to the boil in the 16th century. Disgusted by the offering of bogus 'indulgences', the rebel monk Martin Luther nailed his 95-point thesis to the door of the Wittenberg Palace All Saints' Church in late October 1517. So began the Protestant Reformation, which was to revolutionize Europe. At first Jews welcomed the new religious trend: they were no longer the only non-conformists in Europe, and some imagined that Protestants would be their natural allies. Luther published a pamphlet stressing the links between Jews and

Right *A historical turning point? When thugs looted Frankfurt's Jewish ghetto in 1614, Habsburg Emperor Matthias hanged the instigators and restored Jewish property.*

Christians, called *Christ was Born a Jew*. And while his aim was always to convert Jews, he insisted that this should be done with gentleness.

THE PROTESTANTS TURN

Jews soon learnt Protestants could be just as anti-Semitic as Catholics. When Jews rejected Luther's advances he issued a virulent attack on them in 1543, recommending a programme of arson, expropriation, hard physical labour and ultimately, 'if we are afraid that they may harm us', driving them 'out of the country for all time'.

After reforms in 1356, German emperors had given local princes or imperial 'electors' the right to tax Jews. Once Jews could appeal directly to the emperor; now they had to contend with the whims of local fiefs. Eventually, however, in 1614, Emperor Matthias (r. 1612–19) stood up against anti-Semites and hanged the ringleaders of a pogrom in Frankfurt. He then ceremonially restored the Jews to their homes.

Below *The vast and sprawling Holy Roman empire was generally inhospitable terrain for Jews.*

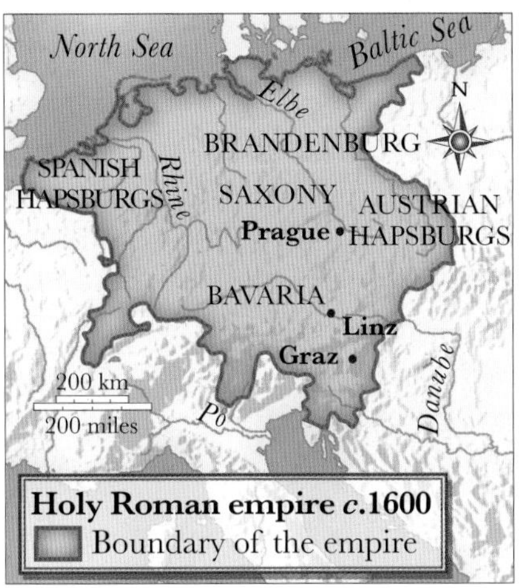

Generally, Jews fared better in the northern German states of the Hanseatic League. Semi-autonomous from the empire, the League afforded opportunities for trade with Scandinavia and the Baltic states. By the 16th century Jews from Spain and Portugal migrated to the region. They soon forged lucrative links with fellow Sephardim in Holland and Ashkenazim in Germany.

THE RISE OF COURT JEWS

Jews also benefited from the Thirty Years War, which erupted in 1618 between the Holy Roman empire and an array of foes, both Catholic and Protestant. Almost single-handedly one Jew, Jacob Bassevi of Prague, saved the imperial Habsburg army from bankruptcy with loans and a food-supply network in eastern Europe. Some Jews profited from supplying the opposition; other Jews became contractors to Swedish forces. In sum, the war brought about two changes. First, Jewish communities who used to suffer from any conflict were now treated better than others. Second, there were 'court Jews' who funded capital projects in peacetime as in war, who advised rulers, and who capitalized on these factors to safeguard the interests of poorer Jews.

Below *This painting by Flemish artist Sebastien Vrancx depicts the Thirty Years War, 1618–48, during which some Jews shrewdly gained influence.*

Jews in the Ottoman Empire

After Muslim Turkey threw Spanish Jews a lifeline in 1492, Sephardim revived Jewish communities across the Ottoman-ruled Balkans, eastern Mediterranean and North Africa.

To the beleaguered Jews in 15th-century Spain, the sight of offshore sailing masts belonging to the Ottoman fleet was particularly reassuring. Between 1490 and 1492 the naval commander Kemal Reis sent ships to hug the Iberian coastline, picking up load after load of refugees and transporting them to Turkey and the Ottoman provinces. Even after Granada fell to Christian Spaniards, Reis bombarded the ports of Almería and Málaga on behalf of fellow Muslims suffering in Spain, and in 1506 he rescued the last consignment of Jews and Arabs who wished to escape the Spanish Inquisition.

BAYEZID'S INVITATION

Whereas Christian nations accepted Jews begrudgingly, Sultan Bayezid II (r. 1481–1512) made it Ottoman policy to welcome them. He was keen to engage worldly-wise entrepreneurs in building up his nascent empire. Adroitly calculating that Christianity's loss could be Islam's gain, he openly invited the Jews to immigrate, and he said of Spain's king, Ferdinand: 'Can you call such a king wise or intelligent? He is impoverishing his country and enriching my kingdom'.

Turkey's existing 50,000 Jews generously helped their brethren, performing 'unlimited great deeds of charity, giving money as if it were stones', reported the chronicler Rabbi Elijah Capsali. About 150,000 arrived, of whom 40,000 settled directly in Constantinople. Jews also came to Salonika in Greece, whose Jewish population rose to 20,000 by 1553; to Izmir (formerly Smyrna); and to Adrianople, now Edirne in European Turkey, site of an earlier influx of Ashkenazim from France and Germany. Adrianople's rabbi, Isaac Sarfati, even posted letters to communities in Hungary, Moravia and the Rhineland praising the liberality of the Sultanate.

Above *Ambassadors paying homage to the Ottoman Sultan Suleiman the Magnificent; from a 16th-century manuscript about his campaigns.*

Once ensconced as citizens of the empire, Sephardi Jews did well, establishing the first Gutenberg press in Constantinople in 1493, and working as skilled craftsmen, iron-casters and makers of gunpowder.

OTTOMAN RULE

During the reign of Suleiman the Magnificent (1520–66) the Ottoman empire controlled Asia Minor, Egypt, North Africa, the eastern Mediterranean and all of the Middle East apart from Persia. In fact the dynasty originated as a small *beylik* (principality) abutting Byzantine territory. After Mongols vanquished Anatolia's powerful Seljuk Turks, the Ottomans began their inexorable rise, led after 1281 by Osman (known as Ottoman to Europeans).

Left *Simple yet dignified, the Etz Hayyim ('tree of life') synagogue in Chania, Crete, a Greek island long under Ottoman control.*

Above *Once a haven for Jews under Turkish rule, Safed houses this synagogue named after a famous rabbinical resident, Joseph Caro.*

The first Jewish community under their control was Bursa in north-west Anatolia, taken in 1326. Osman's son, Orhan, allowed Jews to build the Etz Hayyim (Tree of Life) synagogue, and Jews immigrated from as far as Arabia. In swift succession the Ottomans took over parts of Romania and Bulgaria, Serbia, Albania, Macedonia and Greece, most of which had small Jewish populations.

Having captured Byzantium in 1453, Sultan Mehmet II (1432– 81) confirmed Moses Kapsali as chief rabbi. The Greek-born Kapsali was known for both his impartiality as a civil magistrate and tax supervisor, and also for his friendship with Mehmet and Bayezid II. Scrupulous in matters of religion, he defended normative Judaism against Karaite attack and youthful rebels. Mehmet encouraged Jews from Crete and the provinces to live in Constantinople.

In 1556 he sent a Jewish regiment called 'Sons of Moses' to fight rebel Christian forces in Belgrade. Leading the enemy army was the monk John Capistrano, a notorious persecutor of Jews in Italy, Sicily, Bavaria, Silesia, Austria and Poland.

SEPHARDIM DOMINATION

Supremely confident that they originated from the most refined culture in Europe, Sephardi Jews set up their own synagogues. Soon a familiar pattern was repeated, but with a difference: in the past there had been rivalry between Babylonian rite synagogues and Palestinian; now it was Spanish versus indigenous. Ottoman authorities asked synagogues to collect taxes, so they became fiscal bodies as well as spiritual and communal centres and schools.

In places where each community had its own synagogue (Italian, Sephardi, Ashkenazi, Romaniote), an umbrella *kehillah*, or 'Hebrew community', came to represent them all. Moreover, ad hoc Jewish general assemblies administered internal affairs, while Ottoman Jewish law courts enjoyed more autonomy than their equivalents in Christian Europe. Ottoman prestige rose among European Jews, too, when Palestine fell to Turkish hands in 1516.

JOSEPH CARO

The Ottoman subject who made the greatest impact on Jews was rabbi and mysticist Joseph Caro (1488–1575). He was born in Spain, moved as a child to Portugal and lived in Adrianople, Salonika, Constantinople, Safed and Jerusalem. Probably even more than Moses Maimonides, Caro determined the authoritative code of law and practice for generations of Orthodox Jews. His magnum opus, *Beth Yosef* (House of Joseph) was an overview of 32 authorities on Talmudic rulings. Caro intended to rationalize the rapidly diverging Sephardi and Ashkenazi approaches to law.

His much shorter abridgement of *Beth Yosef*, entitled *Shulkhan Arukh* (Prepared Table), achieved immortality. Published in Venice in 1574, it was to be 'carried in one's bosom and referred to at any time and any place'. Critics found it didactic; Caro himself suggested it was mainly for simpletons or beginners. However, aided by the printing revolution, the 'Table' gained popularity in both Ashkenazi and Sephardi households.

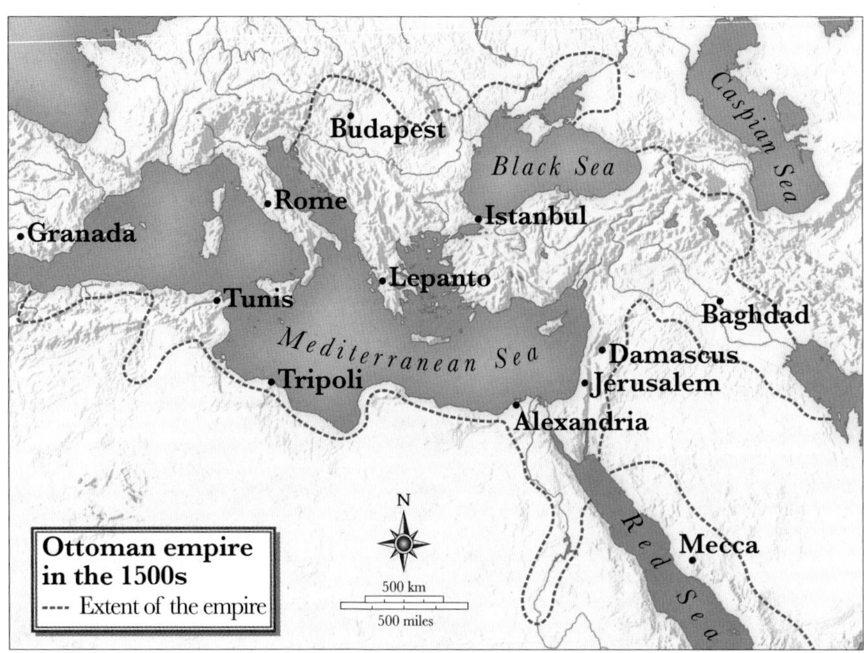

Right *Sephardi Jews breathed new life into the Ottoman empire, which by the 1500s included Jerusalem and Mecca.*

TURKS AND JEWS IN THE HOLY LAND

THE OTTOMANS ELEVATED THE OFFICE OF CHIEF RABBI AFTER TAKING PALESTINE IN 1516, AND ALLOWED JEWS SUCH AS DONA GRACIA HITHERTO UNPARALLELED INFLUENCE IN IMPERIAL AFFAIRS.

Unlike his predecessors who were obsessed with European campaigns, Selim I the Grim (r. 1512–20) turned east after taking the Ottoman throne in 1512. He defeated Shah Ismail of Shia Persia in 1514, took Palestine and Syria in 1516, occupied Egypt in 1517 and gained possession of Arabian territories from the Mamluks.

At a stroke Selim became steward of Islam's three holiest cities – Mecca, Medina and Jerusalem – and declared himself Caliph over all Muslims. Ottoman rule reunited Jewish communities in the Balkans, North Africa and the Middle East. Significantly, from a Jewish perspective, Turks ruled the Land of Israel and Jerusalem, and would do so for another 400 years.

Below Jewish doctors often served the Ottoman court; drawing by the French geographer Nicolas de Nicolay, 1568.

CHIEF RABBI OF THE LEVANT

In 1452 the Ottomans had established the office of chief rabbi, and after 1517 the officeholder became in effect Exilarch of the Levantine Diaspora. Formally this included Palestinian Jews, too. The incumbent rabbi was Elijah Mizrahi, a Romaniote Jew. He was proficient in Arabic, Hebrew, Italian and Greek, wrote a famous commentary on Rashi's Torah, accepted Karaites as students and as a mathematician reputedly discovered how to extract the cube root.

The Ottomans set up the *kakhya*, or 'office for secular administration', headed by Shealtiel, a Turkish-speaking Jew. Jews were recognized as a separate ethno-religious community, alongside Greek Orthodox, Armenian Christians and others. However, Muslims outnumbered the minorities, Jews and Christians had to pay protection and head tax, and the Chief Mufti held a cabinet post, unlike the spiritual leaders of the Christian and Jewish communities.

Generally 16th-century sultans favoured Jews over Christians, and several rose to positions of power, such as Mehmet II's minister of finance, Hekim Yakup Pasha, and Murad II's physician, Ishak Pasha. Selim followed the trend by appointing Abraham Castro master of the mint and *nagid*, or Jewish community leader, in Egypt. Closer ties came during the 1520–66 reign of Suleiman the Magnificent, who rebuilt Jerusalem's city walls. He won popularity when his troops captured Rhodes in 1522, freeing and gaining fighters from 4,000 Jews whom the ruling Knights Hospitaller had been using as slave labourers.

Above Sultan Selim the Grim, who took Palestine and Syria in 1516, thus uniting Eastern Jews under one rule.

FAMILY RELATIONS

The Jewish pair who wielded the most power was Don Joseph Nasi, born as the Portuguese Marano João Micas around 1524, and Dona Gracia, his aunt and mother-in-law. They turned a precious-stones enterprise into a banking empire. Cultured and charming, Gracia left Portugal via England for Antwerp, mingled with European nobles and arrived in Venice in 1545. Turkish diplomats intervened when she was denounced as a Judaizer. She arrived in Constantinople in 1553 and was reunited with her nephew, having arranged escape passages for other Portuguese Maranos.

In Constantinople Don Joseph regularly met foreign ambassadors and counselled sultans on matters of policy, especially concerning the Middle East. He became a *muterferik*, or 'gentleman of the royal retinue', and Duke of the island of Naxos. In 1560, he and Gracia were allowed to develop a Jewish colony at Tiberias, near the Sea of Galilee, to the betterment of all its inhabitants.

Joseph, now Lord of Tiberias, encouraged Suleiman to attack Cyprus, a Venetian possession. At the subsequent naval battle off Lepanto

Above Born in Portugal, Dona Gracia became in her day the most influential woman in the Ottoman empire.

LADINO: THE SEPHARDI LINGUA FRANCA

As Yiddish is to Ashkenazim, so is Ladino to the Sephardi Jews – a much-loved hybrid language filled with pathos, wit and charm. Again, like Yiddish, the number of its speakers has sadly dwindled; only about 80,000 Jews in Israel and a few thousand others outside still understand Ladino. The sole surviving Ladino newspaper is printed in Istanbul (formerly Constantinople).

Also known as Judeo-Spanish, Judezmo, Spanyol, or Haquitiya in Spanish Morocco, the word Ladino derives from 'Latin'. The language is based on medieval Castilian with lashings of Hebrew, Aramaic and a little Turkish, Arabic, French and Italian. Until recently Ladino was written in Hebrew characters, using a cursive 'rabbinic' typeface. Its heyday came after the 1492 expulsion, and the first Ladino Bible translation appeared in the 1700s in Constantinople. The most famous Ladino work was *Me'am Lo'ez* (1730), a retelling of Bible stories. There was a strong oral rather than written culture until the 19th century. Ladino is being revived as a literary language in academic circles and, in a curious reversal of normal practice, it might as a result be catching on again as a spoken language. This is partly driven by a revival in Ladino music.

in 1571, however, a combined fleet of Spanish, Venetian and papal ships humiliated the Ottoman navy. Turkey secured Cyprus in 1573 and Tunis the next year, but Joseph, blamed for his Lepanto miscalculation, was never named king of Cyprus.

JEWISH DIPLOMATS

Turkey used Jews to negotiate with European political figures. Joseph's rival, Solomon Ashkenazi, represented Turkey in peace talks with Catholic Venice, despite Venetian reluctance to meet a Jew. He later got Venice to cancel a threat to expel its Jews. Don Joseph called for an embargo of the Adriatic port of Ancona, after the Inquisition began targeting the Portuguese Maranos living there. The embargo was opposed by Italian Jews who feared papal retribution and ultimately failed. Yet it signalled an early use of economic power as a political weapon.

SAFED VERSUS JERUSALEM

Palestinian Jews benefited economically after the Ottoman conquests of 1516–17. Contacts grew with Jews in Syria and Egypt, and soon 1,500 Jewish families were living in Jerusalem. By the late 16th century some 15,000 Jews were drawn to Safed, both by its holiness and its trade with nearby Damascus. Their prosperity, though, stoked resentment in a poorer Jerusalem.

One wealthy Safed spice dealer, Rabbi Jacob Berab, also harboured millennial ambitions. He wanted to revive the Great Sanhedrin, and persuaded Joseph Caro and others in Safed to reinstate the Temple custom of *smicha*, or 'priestly ordination by the laying on of hands'. But Jerusalem rabbis declared that such practices were forbidden until the Temple was restored.

DECLINE AFTER SULEIMAN

After Suleiman died in 1566, Muslims in Tiberias protested against Jewish plans to build city walls, and local governors imposed burdens on residents, especially Jews. Meanwhile, the Ottoman conquest of Hungary in 1526 had brought thousands of Ashkenazi Jews into the Turkish fold. Most felt comfortable, yet Christians perceived a Muslim threat to their security, and often cast their suspicion at the Ashkenazi population of eastern Europe.

Left A 1517 etching of the Ottoman capture of Erzerum, which opened the gateway to the Middle East.

CHAPTER 2

A CHANGING FAITH

Disasters have typically inspired messianic hopes of redemption among Jews. This was certainly true after Ukrainian pogroms and Polish wars engulfed mid-17th-century Europe. From Cairo to Amsterdam, Jews flocked to the cause of a charismatic rabbi from Turkey named Shabbetai Tzvi, who drew from the mystical Kabbalah tradition of Safed, Palestine.

When Shabbetai proved to be a fraud, new trends emerged to fill the void. One was Hassidism, a return to Orthodox faith infused with spiritual joy that rejected elitism and intellectualism. Another was the Haskalah, a Jewish variant of the European Enlightenment, which defined Jews as a nationality worthy of full civil rights. The Haskalah in turn inspired the modernizing Reform Judaism movement, while revolutions in 18th-century America and France seemed to promise an age of equality. The historian Leopold Zunz said Jews made a dramatic transition from a prolonged Middle Ages straight into the modern era. But when Tsarist Russia corralled Jews from a dismembered Poland into a vast Pale of Settlement, such dreams of tolerance and progress became delusions.

Opposite *A 17th-century Turkish folk art depiction of a rabbi holding a Torah aloft, chanting the traditional words: 'This is the Torah Moses set before the Children of Israel'.*

Above *The First Great Sanhedrin, supreme court of the Jewish people, which Napoleon granted to Jews in France, symbolizing his scheme to be patron of a Jewish national revival.*

A CRISIS OF FAITH

BATTERED BY WARS AND POGROMS IN UKRAINE AND POLAND, EUROPEAN JEWS EAGERLY LOOKED TO TURKISH RABBI SHABBETAI TZVI, ONLY TO DISCOVER HE WAS A FALSE MESSIAH.

From his vantage point in late 16th-century Prague, Rabbi Judah Loew was relieved that the expulsions of the Middle Ages had come to an end. But his optimism was to prove misplaced: at least 100,000 Jews were slaughtered in the Ukraine during 1648–54 in the so-called Chmielnicki massacres. The upheaval also generated impossible messianic expectations, which, once dashed, set Jews back for decades if not centuries.

JEWS BETWEEN TWO FAITHS

Mid-17th-century Europe felt threatened by Muslim Ottomans. The Ottomans had besieged Vienna in 1529 and taken most of Hungary and Transylvania by 1546. They fought Poland to stalemate after a 15-year-long war that ended in 1606, and launched a campaign against Venice in 1645. Many Christians suspected their Jewish neighbours were acting as a Turkish fifth column.

Below: Chief Rabbi Jacob Loew's grave in Prague's Old Jewish Cemetery, Czech Republic, where his nephew Rabbi Judah Loew, the Maharal of Prague, is also buried.

However, the great Ukrainian pogroms arose not out of any Muslim–Christian clash, but from a vicious fight within Christendom. In 1569 the newly created Polish–Lithuanian Commonwealth took over large parts of Ukraine where Catholic Polish landlords encouraged Jews to run their estates. By now some 75 per cent of the world's Jews may have lived in Greater Poland.

But Ukraine's peasants were Orthodox Christian, not Catholic, and felt closer to Russians than to Poles. In addition, the Cossacks of central Ukraine, a militant caste, yearned for independence. Most Ukrainians therefore despised the Polish nobles and hated their Jewish administrators with even greater venom. In 1648 the Cossack commander Bogdan Chmielnicki (*c.* 1595–1657) rebelled against the Polish yoke, telling peasants that the Catholics had sold them 'into the hands of the accursed Jews'. He quickly repulsed Commonwealth forces and declared himself 'sole autocrat of the Rus' in 1649.

Churches were burnt, priests and nobles slaughtered and estates pillaged. Nearly a million are thought to have died. Proportionately, Jews suffered worst, with 300 population centres destroyed and more than 100,000 killed. Though contemporary estimates of up to 500,000 are probably exaggerated, the killings surpassed in brutality the pogroms of the Crusades and of the Black Death, and dispelled illusions that eastern and central Europe had adopted Enlightenment values.

Above Hero to some, villain to many – statue completed in 1888 of Bogdan Chmielnicki, in Kiev, Ukraine.

Tsarist Russia absorbed a weakened Ukraine in 1654 and then attacked Poland. Russian troops killed 100,000 Jews mercilessly during the resultant Russo-Polish war (1654–67). Finally 'The Deluge', or series of 'misfortunes' following the Swedish invasion and occupation of the Polish Commonwealth (1655–60), created yet more havoc.

FLIGHT NORTH AND WEST

The gruesome four-way war between Ukraine, Russia, Poland and Sweden drove thousands of Jews westward, reversing a trend of eastward migration that had prevailed for two centuries. Many Ashkenazi refugees settled in Amsterdam alongside the existing Sephardi community. Others fled to Lithuania in the north, where local communities raised ransoms to redeem fellow Jews kidnapped by Tartars, the temporary allies of the Cossacks.

MESSIANIC STIRRING

Increasingly, Jews turned to mysticism for solace. Could these torments, they wondered, be the apocalypse that preceded the coming of the Messiah? Rumours began to pour in about a Kabbalistic 'system' that explained the mysteries of the world. The creators of this system were Rabbi Isaac Luria (1534–72), a friend of Joseph Caro, and his disciple Haim Vital (1543–1620). Both lived in Safed, in Galilee, the highest city in Ottoman-ruled Palestine and spiritually almost on a par with Jerusalem.

Luria likened the state of exile to *tzimtzum*, or God's 'withdrawal' or 'contraction' from the world at the tumultuous act of creation. Each human soul, he said, contained a *nitzotz*, or 'spark' of the divine. To move from exile to redemption, everyone, and especially Jews, should practise *tikkun olam*, or 'repairing the world', by gathering the sparks that escaped on the first day, according to Genesis. Humanity could thus achieve global harmony, explained Luria, by appeasing God through good acts, or *mitzvot*.

Jews outside Safed began reading into Luria's beliefs a radical explanation and a possible cure for historical disasters. While 'purer' Kabbalists warned against the vulgar mixing of Lurianic mysticism with ideas of a coming saviour, many felt the genie was out of the bottle.

THE FALSE MESSIAH

The man who most dramatically and disastrously inspired public passion was Shabbetai Tzvi, a Sephardi Jew born in Smyrna (Izmir), Turkey, in 1626. The son of a trading agent for Dutch and English firms, Tzvi oscillated between ecstasy and gloom, which would suggest symptoms of extreme manic depression.

Expelled from Smyrna, Salonika and Constantinople, Tzvi fled to Palestine where he visited a Lurianic Kabbalist called Nathan of Gaza (*c.* 1643–80) in the hope of a cure. Instead Nathan, an Ashkenazi, persuaded Tzvi that he was the foretold messianic descendant of David. Together they 'revealed' themselves on 31 May 1665: Tzvi rode around Gaza on horseback, appointing ambassadors to summon the lost tribes of Israel, while Nathan became his prophet and 'holy lamp'.

Jews in Poland, Holland, Germany, Syria, Greece, Egypt and even England were swept up in the year-long, intense craze and spread Tzvi's message. Tzvi returned to Smyrna, broke into the main synagogue and announced the date of redemption – 18 June 1666 – when he would depose the Sultan and divide the world into new kingdoms.

SHABBETAI'S APOSTASY

Nathan announced that the Lurianic system was now overthrown and that Israelite armies were gathering in the Sahara to greet the messiah. Many Jews sold all their goods and did penance in preparation for their 'return to Zion'. Others deliberately contravened the holiest Jewish laws and indulged in sexual lewdness.

__Left__ Shabbetai Tzvi, the false messiah, blessing Jews in Smyrna, Turkey, from a contemporary woodcut, c. 1665.

__Above__ Nathan of Gaza, Shabbetai's chief ally, is blamed for dashing the hopes of a generation of Jews.

Understandably perturbed, Ottoman officials arrested Tzvi when his ship entered Turkish waters, and jailed him in Constantinople. In September 1666 a Polish Kabbalist denounced him as an impostor. Faced with the choice of conversion or death, Shabbetai Tzvi became a Muslim, renamed himself Aziz Mehmed Effendi and was appointed the Sultan's official gatekeeper.

A shocked Jewish world fell suddenly silent, and the Sultan exiled Tzvi to Albania for his safety, where he died in 1676. Shabbateanism survived in pockets thanks to Nathan the master publicist, who explained that Tzvi's apostasy merely disguised his descent into evil to restore the last lost sparks. But most Jews felt badly deceived.

As to why mass obsession took root, it seems that crisis and upheaval so troubled a vulnerable 17th-century group that they readily believed a delusional mystic's utopian promises.

PALESTINE – A MESSIANIC OUTPOST

KABBALAH MYSTICISM DREW JEWS TO 16TH-CENTURY SAFED, YET THEY FORMED A MINORITY OF PALESTINE'S TOTAL POPULATION. WITHIN 300 YEARS, OTTOMAN NEGLECT LED TO ARAB REVOLT.

Perched on a hill overlooking the Sea of Galilee, Safed is one of the four holy cities to Jews, alongside Jerusalem, Hebron and Tiberias. Under Ottoman rule in the 16th century, it rapidly grew into the largest and most developed town in Palestine with the second-largest Jewish population in Asia. It also acted as a magnet for some of the greatest scholars in Jewish history. Here the Kabbalah, the main Jewish mystical tradition, truly developed – a phenomenon that gave comfort and guidance to millions, but also, in the wrong hands, spawned the false messiah movements that imperilled the Jewish faith everywhere.

Below *Ceiling of the Abuhav Synagogue, Safed, built in the 16th century and full of mystical Kabbalistic imagery.*

Right *Mohammed Ali, Pasha of Egypt, whose actions sparked revolt in Palestine after 1834.*

RABBI ISAAC LURIA – THE LION

More than any other, Rabbi Isaac Luria (1534–72) revolutionized Jewish thought with his new system of the Kabbalah. Known as the Ha-Ari, or 'The Lion', he was born in Jerusalem in 1534 to an Ashkenazi father and Sephardi mother. He studied Torah in Egypt, made a living as a spice merchant, and arrived in Safed in 1569 where he studied directly under the great Kabbalist, Moses Cordevero (1522–70). Yet while this teacher was a master of close textual analysis of the Zohar, the prime book of Jewish mysticism, his pupil went in another direction.

EXILE TO REDEMPTION

Rabbi Luria described how in the imperfect world after Creation, the *shekhina*, or 'divine presence', known as the indwelling spirit or the feminine aspect of God, is itself in exile. Redemption would come when exile ended. For many Jewish listeners, such ideas had relevance in the real world and excited messianic expectations. On a national level they suggested there would be a Jewish return to Palestine, or the Land of Israel.

Gentle-natured and intuitive, Luria wanted his doctrines kept secret, in case they were misinterpreted. Luria wrote little himself, but his protégé Haim Vital recorded his thoughts and fashioned Lurianic Kabbalah into an intricate system of moral and spiritual empowerment. After Luria died during an epidemic in 1572, aged 38, his disciples disseminated his works via the printing presses of Safed, Vilna, Constantinople and Livorno.

RISE AND DEMISE OF SAFED

Beyond the mystical, Safed became a thriving industrial centre based on manufactured cloth, which in the still-new Ottoman empire was a novelty. Wool was imported from Macedonia in the Balkans and then shipped to the town of Safed by way of Sidon and Tripoli. In Safed, master weavers turned the wool into cloth that after dyeing was ready for export. Safed families also traded in food and spices with Lebanon and Syria, where there were active Jewish communities. Within Safed, Jews ran a close-knit welfare and administration system that tried to conform to Torah and Talmud precepts.

After the initial boom, problems began to emerge: Safed, like Jerusalem, Tiberias and Hebron, lacked an agricultural hinterland, thus limiting chances of expansion. New sultans neglected provincial towns, and some Turkish or Arab governors of Safed distrusted the town's Jews. Security deteriorated and robbers stalked the highways. In the mid-17th century an influx of zealous Shabbatean devotees, who had given away their worldly belongings, further strained Palestine's battered economy.

Below A 16th-century Torah scroll and traditional casket associated with Rabbi Isaac Luria, in Safed.

Above Johann Gutenberg at work – his printing revolution of 1447 profoundly altered Jewish society too.

ASHKENAZIM IN PALESTINE

Poor Jews in Jerusalem badly needed aid, so *shlichim*, or 'emissaries', were sent from the Holy Land to wealthier Diaspora communities in Alexandria, Constantinople, Izmir and Ashkenazi centres. Diaspora Jews regarded *hallukah*, or 'donating charity', as an honour. Some, such as the esteemed Rabbi Isaiah Horowitz, personally immigrated; he settled in Jerusalem in 1620.

In 1740 the Muslim ruler of northern Palestine invited Haim Abulafia (1660–1744), Rabbi of Izmir, to rebuild the city of Tiberias. That same year the Ottoman Sultan Mahmud I allowed Christians to worship in Jerusalem, and come under the jurisdiction of their European homelands. Perhaps it was this ruling that encouraged more pious Ashkenazim to settle in 'Eretz Israel': first Hasidim from Belarus, Ukraine and Poland, and then, after 1780, Perushim, the 'separated ones' or disciples of the anti-Hassidic Vilna Gaon of Lithuania. By now Jerusalem had eclipsed Safed in importance.

SEEDLINGS OF JEWISH AND ARAB NATIONALISM

As of 1609 Palestine was subsumed within the province of Greater Syria; though Jerusalem was treated as a separate *sanjak*, or a district under a military governor. Most inhabitants of Palestine were neither Turkish nor Jewish, but Sunni Muslim Arabs. Like their Jewish co-residents, Palestinian Arabs loathed the Ottoman tax collectors; unlike them they often protested vigorously.

Their largest revolt came after the Egyptian ruler Mohammed Ali, a former Ottoman vassal, wrested Syria and Palestine from a weakened Turkey in 1831–41. In May 1834 Arab sheikhs from Nablus, Jerusalem and Hebron refused to offer Ali conscripts; they briefly took Jerusalem, Safed, Tiberias and Haifa. Ali and his son, the Egyptian army commander Ibrahim Pasha, eventually crushed the uprising. Arab historians call it the 'Syrian Peasant Revolt', although others detect the first strains of a specifically Palestinian Arab nationalism.

For their part, Jews also harboured nationalist dreams but they felt that return from exile should come from a divine agency. They generally favoured Ottoman rule of law, which helped bind one Diaspora community to another.

JEWS OF NORTH AFRICA AND THE MIDDLE EAST

FROM TIMBUKTU IN AFRICA TO BUKHARA IN CENTRAL ASIA, JEWS WERE DYNAMIC TRADERS, WHILE SEPHARDI IMMIGRANTS REVITALIZED ANCIENT LEVANTINE COMMUNITIES.

The Sephardi Jews who were exiled from the Iberian Peninsula at the end of the 15th century generally felt safe under Ottoman rule. They no longer needed to fear persecution, or hide their identity in public. However, later sultans and governors proved less accommodating than earlier ones, economic slowdown hampered scholastic development, and wars between Europe and Turkey interfered with ties between Jews in both zones. The first challenge facing Sephardim in the 16th century was how to co-exist with the old Jewish communities of North Africa and the Middle East.

Jewish merchants of the Ottoman empire from the 16th to the 19th centuries, transported merchandise to the great cities of Salonika and Constantinople, just as they had done under the Romans 1,500 years earlier. Jews were invaluable to commerce with Europe because many could speak German, French, Italian and Spanish.

Old Jewish firms in Muslim ports like Basra and Alexandria imported foreign products and exported raw materials. New Jewish-run industries, especially weaving, boomed in Salonika, Safed, Izmir and Algiers.

CAIRO

The Ottomans took Cairo in 1517, a year after occupying Jerusalem. There they encountered a mixed Jewish community, which included Sephardi descendants of the 12th-century Spanish scholar Maimonides. Spanish rabbis came to dominate synagogues, with only limited local *mughrabi* opposition. Sultan Selim I (1512–20) appointed Abraham Castro head of the Egyptian mint.

Sephardim settled in Alexandria, Cairo and Rosetta, as well as Damascus and Aleppo in Syria. They founded new yeshivas (rabbinical seminaries); poetry and rabbinic scholarship flourished to the benefit of Egypt and Palestine. Trade was revitalized in the 16th century as peace returned to the eastern Mediterranean and Maghreb (North Africa). Some immigrant Sephardi Jews benefited from the capitulation agreements that Sultan Suleyman (1520–66) signed with Venice and France to protect foreign citizens.

Above *A 19th-century African Mizrah showing the direction of Jerusalem and blending Islamic art and Jewish symbols.*

TUNISIA

Talmudic sages had arrived in Tunisia in the 2nd century and Jews built an esteemed yeshiva in Kairouan soon after Muslim Arabs established it as their fourth holiest city in 670. Spanish raids in the 16th century drove Jews inland and to the mountains, where they took refuge with Berber tribes. Only in the 17th century did Tunisia return to Ottoman control, and even then Tunisian *beys* (governors) enjoyed autonomy.

In the 17th and 18th centuries Italian Jews from Leghorn (Livorno), known colloquially as Grana, joined indigenous Judaeo-Arabic Jews and earlier refugees from Spain in the 'Berber states' of Tunisia, Algeria and

Left *Lighting the candles in the ancient El-Ghriba synagogue on the Tunisian island of Djerba.*

Right Jewish Wedding in Morocco, *Eugène Delacroix, 1841.*

Tripolitana (part of today's Libya). They were very European in their dress, attire, speech and habits. In Tunisia they enjoyed the company of the forcibly converted Spanish Muslims who were expelled from Spain in 1609, and who, like the Grana, spoke Spanish.

By contrast, the Jews of the island of Djerba claim descent from Israelites who fled Babylonian persecution. They held to customs that probably originated in First Temple times. Their El-Ghriba Synagogue, the oldest in Africa, is still active and attracts Jews and other pilgrims.

JOURNEY TO TIMBUKTU

Evidently, a thriving Jewish community once existed in the vital trading entrepôt of Timbuktu, Mali. Southern Moroccan Jews imported gold and salt from inner Africa through the city, and many settled there, including Sephardi refugees from Spain. Most later converted to Islam, though pockets remain who proudly recall their Jewish roots and are reviving Judaic traditions in the 21st century.

Below *Jewish children in Hara Sghira, Tunisia, learn the Hebrew alphabet.*

YEMEN

Jews were already established in Yemen in the 5th century, and in medieval times regularly sought rulings from Maimonides when he lived in Fustat in Cairo. Jews in Sana'a, the capital, kept close contact with the academies in Iraq. The port of Aden also became a vital transit point for lucrative Jewish trade with India.

The Turks conquered Yemen in 1546, but soon lost control of Sana'a to local sheikhs and Zaydi Shia imams who accused the Jews of helping the foreigners. During this period of incessant revolts and forced conversions, the great Yemenite Jewish poet Shalom Shabazi wrote his finest works, such as *Im Nin 'Alu* and *As'alk.*

PERSIAN JEWRY

Shia Persia lay outside the Ottoman realm, and resisted the Constantinople Caliphate's presumption to represent all Muslims. Many Persian Jews had generally suffered under the Shia regimes of the Safavid dynasty, so they welcomed the new Sunni dynast, Nadir Shah (1736–47). He settled numerous Jews in Mashad, a city where the community thrived as rug merchants. They bolstered state coffers by trading in silk and gems with other Jews in Mirv, Khiva, Samarkand and Bukhara in Central Asia, and Herat in Afghanistan. Many thousands migrated to these imperial outposts as well as to Kurdistan, Egypt and India. Politically, Persian Jews served as negotiators between Sunni Turkestanis and Shia Iranians and had their own representatives in local government.

The fragility of Persian Jewish life was shown when the Qajar dynasty, which ruled Iran from 1796 until 1921, restored Shia ascendancy. They persecuted minorities and in 1839 – a century after Nadir Shah – forced the Jews of Mashad to convert to Islam. Elsewhere Jews were quarantined in separate neighbourhoods.

Paradoxically, Qajar excesses attracted the attention of Jews in the West who threw lifelines to their brethren in Persia. In 1865 French Jews represented by the educational association Alliance Israelite Universelle, and Sir Moses Montefiore, an influential English Sephardi philanthropist, interceded with ministers in Tehran to better the lot of Persian Jewry. This pattern was repeated in Ottoman territories.

Despite a promising start at the beginning of the 16th century, therefore, the Sephardim had to call on all their resources of ingenuity and perseverance to survive in often unstable conditions in North Africa and the Middle East over two centuries.

Revolutionary Times

DESPITE THEIR SMALL NUMBERS AND ALMOST ACCIDENTAL ORIGINS, JEWS FOUGHT IN AMERICA'S 1776 WAR OF INDEPENDENCE. SOON AFTERWARDS, THE FRENCH REVOLUTION ENCOURAGED HOPE IN THE OLD WORLD, TOO.

Today the United States of America houses seven million Jews, the largest single Jewish community in the world. By contrast there were barely 2,000 Jews in North America when English settlers declared their independence from Britain in 1776.

NEW WORLD STIRRINGS

A desire for liberty inspired the earliest Jewish migrants to North America. Jews were admitted as burghers (town citizens) and in 1654 they set up their first congregation, She'arit Israel, or 'Remnant of Israel', in New Amsterdam. The city was renamed New York in 1665, and ceded to the English in 1674.

Meanwhile, Rhode Island, founded as an outpost of religious freedom in 1643, attracted 15 Sephardi families from the West Indies to its leading town, Newport, in 1658. Almost immediately they set up Congregation Jeshurat Israel and built the first permanent synagogue in North America in 1763. It was named Touro after its dynamic spiritual leader, Isaac Touro.

Below *Touro Synagogue, Rhode Island, built in 1763 and the oldest Jewish house of worship in the USA.*

Right *John Adams, a founding father of the USA, whose ambiguous views on Jews reflected that of many Americans.*

OLD TESTAMENT PURITANS

Mid-18th-century North America was a patchwork quilt of mostly coastal European colonies – French, Spanish, English, Swedish and Dutch – dotted among a majority population of Native Americans. Most of the English settlers were devout Nonconformist Protestants called Puritans, and although there were hardly any Jews among them, they felt strongly attached to Jewish mores. They likened their departure from England to the flight of the Israelites from Egypt, with the king cast as pharaoh and America as the Promised Land. Hebrew was widely taught at Yale, Harvard and Princeton universities, and nearly half the 1655 legal code of New Haven quoted from the Hebrew Bible, or Old Testament.

SEEDS OF REVOLUTION

English settlers steadily edged out European rivals, especially after New England colonies united as the Massachusetts Bay Colony in 1691. However, tensions with the mother country culminated in the 1773 tax revolt known as the Boston Tea Party, and finally the Declaration of Independence of 1776. Jews fought on both sides in the resulting war, but overwhelmingly for the rebels. As a community, Jews anticipated more freedom to worship, less interference and better opportunities away from the monarchy.

GUARANTEES OF FREEDOM

Pious and God-fearing though America's founding fathers were, their constitution chose to separate church from state and guaranteed freedom of worship. Legislation did not mention Jews specifically, which was almost an advantage. In Europe, 'enlightened despots' were pushing through supposedly emancipating

THE REFORM MOVEMENT

THE 19TH-CENTURY MOVEMENT CALLED REFORM JUDAISM MARKED THE MOST RADICAL DEPARTURE FROM TRADITIONAL JEWISH BELIEF AND PRACTICE TO DATE, AND SPREAD FROM GERMANY TO ENGLAND AND THE USA.

Above *Abraham Geiger, Reform rabbi pioneer and expert on Judaic influence on Christianity and Islam, 1865.*

Reform developed out of Haskalah and aimed to integrate Jews into Europe, bring Judaism up to date with scientific developments and win back those who felt alienated from traditional religion. The idea was to jettison 'obsolete' ritual such as dress codes that attracted suspicion from outsiders, while maintaining and promoting Judaism's ethical core. Reform was thus a natural and perhaps inevitable response to long-brewing cultural developments in Western Jewish society.

NEW METHODS

Reform Jews held services in local vernacular languages. They called their synagogues temples and imitated churches by using choirs and music. Men and women were seated together in prayer, not divided by a *mechitza*, or 'barrier', or segregated into upper and lower floors.

Services were generally shorter and more disciplined affairs than those held in traditional 'shuls' or 'shtiebls'. The centrepiece was a sermon delivered by a rabbi attired in churchlike garb. As in a church, the pulpit assumed prominence.

DOCTRINAL REVOLUTION

Reform abandoned what it saw as obsolete laws that only applied in Temple times. Followers questioned that the Torah came from heaven and they rejected the belief in a personal Messiah, resurrection of the dead, return to the Holy Land and the rebuilding of the Temple. They emphasized the prophetic and lyrical (psalm) tradition rather than the legalistic Talmud and Pentateuch.

Reformists also saw Jews as loyal citizens of their states, rather than as a nation in exile.

THE SPREAD OF REFORM

Israel Jacobsohn was the first rabbi to introduce ceremonial reforms in a synagogue established at Seesen, Germany, in 1810. Another pioneer institution was the Hamburg Temple of 1818. Samuel Hirsch gave the movement a philosophical basis, and the great Haskalah scholar Abraham Geiger lent his support. Perhaps the most important Reform journal was *Allgemeine Zeitung des Judenthums*, edited by Ludwig Philippson.

Although mainly an Ashkenazi phenomenon, Reform appealed to those Sephardi Jews detached from traditional practices. The first Reform synagogue in London began as a breakaway from the Sephardi flagship synagogue, Bevis Marks, in 1841. Other synagogues appeared in Bradford and Manchester, and Reform spawned satellite congregations in Hungary and the USA where it is now the largest US Jewish denomination.

Below *Shielded from street view, as then required by Austrian law, and built in 1824–6, Vienna's Stadttempel (city temple) later adopted the Reform liturgy.*

DEBATE AND CRITICISM

At German Rabbinical conferences in the 1840s a split developed between those who wanted profound change and a majority who worried that Reform was becoming estranged from mainstream Jews. One prominent radical was Samuel Holdheim (1806–60), whose Berlin temple transferred the Sabbath from Saturday to Sunday to match Christian practice. Most congregations decided not to go so far. Some traditionalists, now defined as Orthodox, feared that Reform was halfway towards conversion to Christianity or lapsing into atheism.

In between the two poles were responses that adopted certain Reform features – such as a quizzical attitude to divine authorship. Examples include the Neo-Orthodox school of Samson Raphael Hirsch in Frankfurt, the Neologs in Hungary, and, later, the US Conservative and Reconstructionist (synagogue) trends.

Jews and Commerce – The Rothschilds

In the 19th century the Rothschild name exemplified wealth and success, and so it remains today. Their story is only one chapter in the story of Jewish financial prowess.

From modest origins in the back streets of 18th-century Frankfurt am Main the Rothschild family rose to become the byword for financial ingenuity and commercial success worldwide. Apart from their original banking venture the family's interests have embraced such diverse fields as art patronage, politics, diplomacy, textiles, scientific innovation, oil exploration, engineering works, wine-making and philanthropy. And, while the Rothschild saga is exceptional, it throws light on the challenges and achievements of other Jewish enterprises, large and small.

THE FIRST ROTHSCHILD

The story begins with Mayer Amschel Rothschild (1744–1812), a coin and art dealer who was appointed Crown Agent to the Principality of Hesse-Hanau in 1769. In 1785 Mayer's employer, Prince William, inherited the largest private fortune in Europe. In time Mayer used his hard-won post to launch his own career in banking after working at the Oppenheim banking house in Hanover. By 1785 he could afford a large house, which he shared with his wife, Guttele Schnapper, and their five sons.

Below *Five sons of Mayer Rothschild, each of whom ran a bank branch in a major European financial centre.*

In the early 1800s Mayer expanded his business and set up interdependent banking branches in five major cities, as a deliberate policy of spreading influence and facilitating pan-European links. One son headed each branch: Frankfurt, Vienna, London, Naples and Paris. The bank adopted a crest showing five arrows shooting out in different directions.

INDEPENDENT FINANCIERS

Initially the Rothschilds followed the example of earlier court Jews, like the Wertheimers and Oppenheimers, except that they spread their interests and acted independently, not so much servants of a prince but masters of their own affairs.

By transcending borders while keeping the business within the family, the Rothschilds arguably founded the first transnational corporation. Thus they insured themselves against the dangers of a change of ruler, as had happened in 1737 when Joseph Oppenheimer's patron, Duke Karl Alexander of Wurttemberg, died and jealous rivals sent Joseph to the gallows the next year.

The Rothschilds' early achievements owe much to a happy twist of fate: the moving of the Anti-Napoleonic League's financial centre to Frankfurt from Amsterdam, which had fallen to France. After the Congress of Vienna (1815), which marked Napoleon's defeat by English and Prussian forces, the Rothschilds extended their business into most European states. They made loans to governments, issued state bonds, liquidated inflated paper currencies, founded floating public debts and funded post-Napoleonic war (1815) reconstruction projects. The Austrian emperor made all five brothers peers by 1822, and from 1815 to 1828 their capital rose from 3.2 million francs to 118.4 million.

Above *Baron Lionel de Rothschild, banker, and first professing Jew elected to Britain's parliament, 1836.*

ENGLISH BRANCH

Nathan Mayer Rothschild played a pivotal role in his family's banking success, though he was originally sent to Manchester as a textile merchant in 1798, aged 21. He sold English cloth to Europe until Napoleon's blockade threatened English exports. In 1811 he founded the brokering house N.M. Rothschild. The Rothschild family was soon handling most English financial dealings with the Continent. Nathan's branch funded the British war effort against Napoleon and supplied Wellington's troops with gold before the Battle of Waterloo in 1815.

Between 1818 and 1835 Nathan Mayer issued 26 British and foreign government loans. In 1824 he floated the Alliance Assurance Company and the following year he helped the Bank of England avoid a liquidity crisis. His own dedication to work was legendary and his marriage to the well-connected Hannah Barent Cohen afforded him a network of business contacts. Like his father he was famously discreet, and used similarly cautious agents to courier funds through Napoleonic France. Above all, he understood the value of accurate and speedy information. His private intelligence service learnt the outcome of the Battle of Waterloo a day before the British Government.

Two of Nathan's descendants were path-breakers in British politics, the first being Lionel de Rothschild, who in 1858 became the first professing Jew to enter parliament. In fact, he was first elected in 1847, 11 years earlier, but he refused to take the Christian oath of entrance and so was barred from the chamber. Only when parliament allowed him to swear on the Hebrew Bible did he take his seat. In 1885 Sir Nathan Mayer Rothschild II entered the House of Lords as the first Jewish peer and established a baronetcy in his family's name.

Below The Rothschild Family at Prayer *by the German Jewish painter Moritz Daniel Oppenheim.*

Right *Waddesdon Manor, Buckinghamshire, the Rothschild country estate built 1874–89.*

THE INDUSTRIALISTS

The Rothschilds realized the potential of technological innovation. Salomon Rothschild (1774–1855), head of the Vienna banking branch, built Austria's first railway system. James Mayer de Rothschild (1792–1868), founder of the French branch, played a dominant role in transforming 19th-century France into a major industrial power. He financed mining enterprises and helped found the French railway consortium Chemin de Fer du Nord in 1845. Other Rothschilds backed the newly formed mining conglomerate Rio Tinto Zinc in 1873 and advanced the British Government the money needed to purchase the Suez Canal in 1875.

BEYOND BANKING

Nathan's son Nathaniel (1812–70) moved to Paris, set up a second French branch and acquired a vineyard whose Château Mouton Rothschild wines are among the best in the world.

After the Russian pogroms of the 1880s, Baron Edmond James de Rothschild (1845–1934) set up the Jewish Colonization Association that established 12 settlements in Palestine. Baron Lionel Walter Rothschild was the addressee of the 1917 Balfour Declaration that committed Britain to establishing a 'national home for the Jewish people' in Palestine.

VENTURE CAPITALISTS IN A CHANGING WORLD

Apart from the Rothschilds, Jewish families such as the Warburgs, Mendelssohns and Bleichroeders pioneered merchant banking to meet changing economic needs. Railways were a fruitful source of enterprise: during 1850-70 Samuel Poliakov developed Russia's network, while the Paris-based Maurice de Hirsch (1831–1896) made a fortune in Turkey, Austria and the Balkans. Jews also capitalized American railroads and developed joint stock institutions such as Deutsche Bank, founded in 1870.

Such entrepreneurship built on older traditions of financial innovation. In medieval Baghdad and Cairo Jews had devised *jahbadhiyya*, a system that distributed risk by tying state loans to the savings of the entire Jewish merchant class. Spanish Jews spread to Venice and France other Islamic ideas, such as the cheque (*sakh*) and bill of exchange (*suftaya*). Jewish refugees boosted the prosperity of 16th-century Livorno, Italy, as well as Marseilles, Bordeaux and Rouen in 17th- and 18th-century France. The Henriques family helped found the Bank of England in 1694 and the Ashkenazi Goldsmid banking family joined their Sephardi brethren in the City of London.

In time other Jews realized the potential of a consumer culture. Levi Strauss (1829–1902) invented denim jeans in the US and built a thriving textile business; while in Manchester, England, the Belarus-born Michael Marks (1859–1907) and gentile Thomas Spencer formed in 1894 Marks & Spencers, one of the first major retail chains.

CHAPTER 3

REVOLUTION AND EMANCIPATION

While Jewish civil emancipation proceeded at a snail's pace after the 1815 Congress of Vienna, access to education created a generation of individual Jews whose contributions to art, music, science and politics became considerable. By the late 19th century formal emancipation was achieved, but anti-Semitic factions still survived. Within the community, Orthodox and conservative leaders worried that new liberties might encourage total assimilation, even the disappearance of Judaism itself. Meanwhile in eastern Europe, Jews lacked the opportunities enjoyed in Paris, Berlin or London. Thousands of Russian and Polish Ashkenazi Jews left for America, the 'golden land'. Likewise, Sephardi Jews began deserting an Ottoman empire in decline. Of the Jews who stayed behind, many believed that the betterment of their people was impossible until the whole of society changed. Jews thus flocked to ideologies including Marxism, socialism, and nationalism. Gradually a new strand emerged, Zionism, which sought to 'solve the Jewish problem' by transplanting Diaspora Jews back to the historic Land of Israel, in Palestine.

Opposite An Ashkenazi Rabbi of Jerusalem, *by G.S. Hunter. As the 19th century unfolded, figures of Orthodoxy came under attack from within the Jewish community.*

Above *A bustling street scene in New York, 1890s. Jewish immigrants from Russia and Poland flocked to the city that seemed to offer a chance for new beginnings.*

THE OSTJUDEN AND YIDDISH CULTURE

YIDDISH, THE LANGUAGE OF ASHKENAZIC JEWRY, BECAME THE CHIEF VEHICLE FOR SPREADING INFORMATION IN JEWISH EASTERN EUROPE. IT WAS THE GLUE THAT BOUND A SECULAR SENSE OF 'JEWISHNESS', CALLED *YIDDISHKEIT*.

In western Europe, Yiddish was increasingly regarded as uncouth; the *maskilim*, or 'enlightened ones', of the Jewish Haskalah, spoke German or French among themselves, and wrote learned books in 'purer' Hebrew. By the 20th century, certain elements in Western Jewry professed disdain for the *Ostjuden*, or 'Eastern Jews', under the Russian yoke.

A minority, though, felt nostalgia and even envy towards their Eastern cousins who seemingly maintained a surer sense of who they were, for all their poverty and political deprivation. Some of the most Jewishly creative places in Europe were precisely those areas where *Ostjuden* and refined Western *maskilim* met, such as the 'borderland' cities of Vienna and Budapest in the Austro-Hungarian empire.

Below Red Guards, Moscow, 1917. At first, many Jews welcomed the Russian Revolution as a chance for change.

MATURATION OF HASSIDISM

Once dismissed as a passing phase, Hassidism (a populist expression of Jewish Orthodoxy) had put down deep roots in eastern Europe by the 19th century. Most sects were usually headed by a *rebbe*, or rabbinic 'master', whose authority often overruled that of the local town rabbi.

Hassidic ways had economic implications, as ordinary followers set up mutual self-help societies and funded *tzadikim*, 'righteous ones' who claimed to mediate between God and the common people. Hassidism entered the USA with the great immigration wave of the 1880s, but the movement found unfertile ground. Many Jewish newcomers welcomed America's freedom from European strictures, whether these were official, anti-Semitic or religious. Only much later did New York become the main destination for Hassidic survivors of the Holocaust.

Above Russia before the Revolution. Jews attacked by Russian thugs, 1903, from a contemporary Italian newspaper.

EASTERN EUROPE

The prevailing ethos east of the Dnieper River was more traditional, but eventually the *haskalah* (Jewish enlightenment), spread from its birthplace in Prussia to Austrian Galicia (culturally Polish Jewish) and on to Tsarist Russia. Eastern Haskalah assumed its own distinct character: rather than attempting to reform Judaism or seek political emancipation – a hopeless cause in Russia – Eastern *maskilim* (Haskalah enthusiasts) concentrated on regenerating their communities on a secular basis.

By the late 19th century some Western Jews, who had felt it their duty to educate the Ostjuden about civilized practices, hired east European *maskilim* to teach their children the rudiments of Judaism. Eastern Haskalah served as a bridge to a West that was losing connection with the wellsprings of Jewish tradition.

THE MAY LAWS

Optimists thought that Russia was becoming more liberal when, in 1862, Jews gained equal rights

Right *Klezmer bands were a regular fixture of Ashkenazi life in both eastern Europe and America. This one stands ready at a welcoming party,* c.*1920.*

in Congress Poland, which essentially had been a semi-autonomous puppet state under Tsarist rule since 1815. However, both Poles and Jews suffered when Russia crushed a revolt and incorporated Poland more firmly into the Tsarist realm three years later. Much worse was to follow under Tsar Alexander III (r. 1881–94). Pogroms erupted throughout western Russia and Ukraine and dragged on for three years. Although the authorities did not officially encourage the violence, they did little to stop it.

RADICALIZATION IN RUSSIA

New pogroms, anti-Jewish mass attacks, erupted in 1903–6, coinciding with the abortive 1905 revolution, and yet another wave occurred in 1918–20, during the civil war that followed the Bolshevik Revolution. All told, tens of thousands of Jews died in the period to 1920, during which time two million Jews chose to emigrate, mostly to the USA.

For those who remained in Russia, radicalism set in. Broadly they joined one of four groups: universalist and atheist Marxists; Narodni peasant revolutionaries (who generally did not welcome Jews); the Bund, an all-embracing Russian socialist association specifically for Jewish concerns; or Zionists who laboured for an emancipated Jewish society only in Palestine.

HUNGARY – BETWEEN TWO WORLDS

The distinct worlds of Western Jewry and the Ostjuden touched in Hungary, a land living partly in the shadow of Austria, and blessed with a vast variety of Jewish types: Carpathian mountain Jews, urban German speakers, and Orthodox Jews who preferred speaking Hungarian to Yiddish. Despite enduring residual prejudices from gentile Magyar nationalists, the Jewish population grew and fostered ties with Jews in neighbouring Serbia and Bosnia.

Hungarian Jews took advantage of the 1783 Edict of Tolerance, the brainchild of Emperor Joseph II (1765–90), and entered universities in search of secular education. Hungary's still-small Jewish population was replenished by the influx of Jews from Poland, Slovakia and Moravia. By the end of the 19th century, some 350 Jews had joined the titled nobility. A quarter of all university students and more than 40 per cent of Hungarian bankers, intelligentsia and artists were Jews, even though they made up just 5 per cent of the general population.

City dwellers favoured Reform practices, imported from Germany; and some Orthodox concocted a Hungarian moderate version of reform called Neolog. By contrast, Hassidic sects separated themselves to safeguard Jewish tradition. They set up dynasties in several towns and introduced a new flavour to Hungarian Jewry.

Meanwhile, in Austro-Hungarian Bohemia, Jews thrived because of the combined effect of the Industrial Revolution and weak local nobility. Families such as the Porges built cotton, calico and linen printing factories and spawned Jewish banking clans in Vienna. In the 1840s the Emperor ennobled the Porges, a sign that economic success could bring social respectability without any need to convert from the Jewish faith.

LITERATURE IN YIDDISH

East European Jews took to literature and theatre with alacrity. They wrote mainly in Yiddish, so their output was for Jewish 'domestic consumption'. Early pioneers included the playwright Solomon Ettinger (1802–56) and folklorist S. Ansky (1863–1920), who built on Ostjuden oral story-telling traditions. Ansky's 1914 Yiddish play *The Dybbuk* has been dubbed an Ashkenazi *Frankenstein* and a metaphor for the nature of Jewish life. He also wrote in Russian, while his contemporary Israel Zangwill (1824–1926) used English. Both men's use of the locally dominant language demonstrated the speed of Jewish acculturation. Yet they preserved a sense of Ostjuden culture.

The Spectre of Anti-Semitism Revived

Hopes for Jewish emancipation in Russia were suddenly dashed by an outbreak of violence after 1881. Even in the West, medieval suspicions about Jews revived.

The 1881 pogroms in Russia altered Jewish history profoundly. They were to lead to the birth of political Zionism – the campaign to create a Jewish national state in Palestine – and the growth of American Jewry. They also led indirectly to the Russian Revolution. However, as an instance of official and popular anti-Semitism, the pogroms were not unique.

ATTACK FROM THE RIGHT

Rightists still feared that Jews were eternal aliens. Even the supposedly enlightened Frederick the Great of Prussia decreed in 1750 that 'extra-ordinary' Jews (such as Court Jews) could not pass on their privileges to the next generation. 'Ordinary' Jews were barred from professions, and could not allowed to marry or settle in further numbers 'until a careful investigation [had] been made'.

Below The Dreyfus affair of 1894 exposed an underlying cultural anti-Semitism that shocked French liberals.

In France, Edouard Drumont published a two-volume racist book, *La France Juive* (1886) whose popularity encouraged him to found the Anti-Semitic League and a daily paper, *La Libre Parole* (1896).

Envy of successful Jewish families such as the Reinachs (who included prize-winning lawyers, politicians, archaeologists and classicists) fuelled French rightist dislike for Jews. A string of malicious conspiracy theories followed the Comptoire d'Escompte banking crisis (1889) and the Panama corruption scandal (1893), which both involved Jews.

ANTI-SEMITISM ON THE LEFT

Diverse groups castigated Jews on economic grounds. In 1891 the Russian Jewish thinker Leon Pinsker noted: 'For property holders, [the Jew is] a beggar; for the poor, an exploiter and a millionaire'.

Some radicals saw Jews as financial protectors of oppressive state structures and nobles. Late 19th-century Russian Narodniks and anarchists jointly attacked nobles and *Zhids* (pejorative Russian for Jews). Often there was a nationalist element at play.

THEOLOGY AND SCIENCE

Theologically, some atheists and secularists blamed Jews, the first monotheists, for all the evils of religion. Enlightenment thinkers of the 18th century set this trend when they criticized Jewish beliefs, in what might have been an attack on Christianity itself. The charges stuck, and a century later fused with a new strand of racial anti-Semitism, to emerge as an offshoot of social Darwinism.

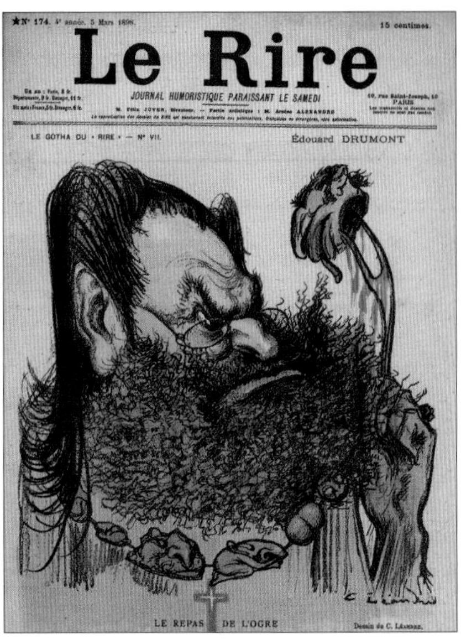

Above Caricature of notorious French anti-Semite Edouard Drumont, from a French satirical journal, 1893.

Ernest Renan, a French philosopher and analyst of religion and nationality, along with like-minded academics, saw Semites in general and Jews in particular as an 'incomplete race' with an 'inferior level of human nature'.

GENTILE FRIENDS

To balance the record of anti-Semitism, Jews also found allies, especially in Britain, such as the parliamentarian and historian Thomas Macaulay, and Walter Scott, whose 1820 novel *Ivanhoe* sympathizes with the plight of Jews in medieval England. Lord Byron's 1815 book of songs, *Hebrew Melodies*, praises Jews' persistence despite exile; and was set to music by a Jewish composer, Isaac Nathan, called the 'father of Australian music'.

Inspired after meeting a learned book cataloguer at the British Library, George Eliot took lessons in Hebrew, visited Palestine in 1869 and often frequented synagogues. Her last novel, *Daniel Deronda* (1878), features an admiring portrayal of a fictitious Jew who rediscovers his identity; his yearning for, and eventual return to,

Palestine inspired many Jews to become Zionists. Similar themes appeared in Prime Minister Benjamin Disraeli's novels *Alroy* and *Tancred*.

PROTECTING JEWS' RIGHTS
The murder of a French capuchin friar in Damascus in 1840 (the Damascus Blood Libel) led to the torture and death of three Jews. Two prominent Jews, Sir Moses Montefiore and Adolphe Crémieux, intervened to stop more bloodshed. The affair led to the creation of the Alliance Israélite Universelle in 1860, a coalition dedicated to safeguarding Jewish rights worldwide.

RUSSIAN RESTRICTIONS
Despite the positive movements of Alliance Israélite, the Tsar's May Laws of 1882 re-imposed cruel restrictions on Russian Jews. They were prevented from entering secondary schools, universities and mining institutes, and were dismissed from government services. These laws, whose prime instigator was Konstantin Pobedonostsev, revealed both economic envy and religious prejudice. They stayed on the statute books until 1907 and provided the basis for other acts of discrimination. In 1886, fines were imposed on Jewish families whose sons failed to report for military service; in 1888 Tsar Alexander III (r. 1881–94) rejected recommendations to extend Jewish rights; and in 1891, 20,000 legally resident Jewish artisans were expelled from Moscow.

Considered together, legislation and pogroms encouraged the greatest movement of Jews to date: between 1881 and 1920, two million Jews left Russia. Some went to Palestine, others to Britain, but overwhelmingly they settled in the United States.

Above French poor hitting a Jewish capitalist, probably a response to the Panama affair, 1893.

So, paradoxically, the Russian laws encouraged the still-nascent Zionist movement, and they also quite unintentionally gave birth to the modern American Jewish community, which in the 20th century became by far the largest and most influential in the world. Within Russia they radicalized more secular-minded Jews, and thus contributed to the revolutions of 1905 and 1917.

THE DREYFUS AFFAIR
The Jews of France felt more secure than most as the 19th century drew to a close. However, in 1894 a Jew from Alsace, Col. Alfred Dreyfus, was falsely accused of betraying military secrets to Germany, and convicted of treason. The trial created an uproar, pitting pro-Dreyfus liberals and republicans, notably the campaigning journalist Emile Zola, against anti-Dreyfus clerics and the social and political old guard. It took 12 years before Dreyfus was exonerated and freed from exile on Devil's Island, by which time France had passed pivotal legislation separating church from state, and safeguarding civil rights.

PROTOCOLS OF THE ELDERS OF ZION

'The Protocols of the Elders of Zion' is one of the most potent, influential and longest-lasting of anti-Semitic tracts. It was a forgery concocted by Russian secret police in the late 19th century and based on the wording of a pamphlet directed against Napoleon III, originally written by a French lawyer, Maurice Joly, in 1864. The Protocols pretends to be a master-plan by secret Jewish leaders plotting to undermine all other nations, socially, morally, economically and politically. Though reprinted during the 1905 Russian Revolution, it reached its peak of popularity during World War I and the 1917 Bolshevik Revolution, when rightists persuaded themselves that Communism was entirely a Jewish conspiracy. The document was disseminated in France by clerics who feared Jewish and Masonic influence; and in England where *The Times* launched an investigation into its authenticity in 1920. From the foundation of the independent State of Israel in 1948 it gained a readership in the Arab world, as a putative 'explanation' of Zionism. Indeed, it is probably no coincidence that its original publication coincided with the first Zionist conference in Basel, Switzerland, in 1897. Philip Graves, a reporter for *The Times*, exposed the forgery in 1921.

Above Illustration of Jew with snakes for hair from 1937 Protocol, a forgery that revealed a supposed Jewish plot to control the world.

THE 19TH-CENTURY POPULATION BOOM

Above Roman Vishniac's 1930s photograph of a heder, or religious class typical of those in eastern Europe.

AN EXTRAORDINARY GROWTH IN JEWISH POPULATION OCCURRED IN THE 19TH CENTURY. BY 1880 THERE WERE AROUND 7.7 MILLION JEWS IN THE WORLD, MOSTLY IN RUSSIA, ALTHOUGH INCREASINGLY IN THE USA.

Improved health standards, high birth rates, better nutrition and relative peace in central and eastern Europe probably accounted for the unprecedented increase in Jewish numbers during the 19th century. As of 1880, nine-tenths of the world's Jews lived in Europe. Around 3.5 million dwelt in the former Polish provinces under Russian rule. The first Russian empire census of 1897 recorded 5.2 million Jews, of whom all but 300,000 still lived in the Pale of Settlement. Another 1.3 million lived in Poland proper, where they made up 14 per cent of the population.

Ashkenazim thus outnumbered Sephardim and Mizrahim (oriental Jews) by a ratio of 9:1. There was also growth in western European Jewry.

Below: Jewish neighbourhood, Lower East Side, New York, c.1900. Eastern European Jews transplanted their culture to an American urban setting.

WESTERNIZATION

In 1820 some 223,000 Jews lived in Germany, but while that represented a significant rise on previous years, the biggest shift of all began 60 years later, in the USA. There the population rocketed, rapidly turning America into an important new centre in Jewish life. Most of the two million Jews who left Tsarist Russia settled there. In the first 15 years of the 20th century, Jews accounted for 10 per cent of all immigrants to the United States. Jewish Americans numbered 2.5 million in 1914.

By then, a quarter of all Jews in the world lived in 11 cities. By far the largest population lived in New York, with an astonishing 1.35 million Jews. London, another immigrant magnet, had more than 150,000. That left sizeable urban communities in other American and European cities including Chicago, Warsaw and Vienna. Occupational expectations gradually changed: the grandparents' generation tended to be Torah observant Jews who worked in small trades as salesmen, cobblers or tailors. Parents took advantage of new freedoms and economic expansion to run larger-scale enterprises, often in mass retailing. But genuine social respectability arrived with the third generation, when their children went to university and became lawyers, accountants or doctors.

IMMIGRANT IDENTITIES

Immigrant Jews of the first two generations cherished their membership of institutions called *landsleitsverreine*, or 'fellow countrymen associations'. Jews from certain towns, such as Krakow, would gather together, in their new cities. By the third generation, however, bonds to the old country had weakened, and Yiddish gave way to English in the USA, Canada, Australia and South Africa, or Spanish in Argentina and Mexico. Now Jewish immigrants felt equally American (or Australian or Chilean) and Jewish, but no longer so strongly Litvak (Lithuanian Jewish), say, or Polack (Polish Jewish).

THE USA – A NEW PROMISED LAND

WHEN EARLY 20TH-CENTURY YIDDISH WRITERS SPOKE OF *DI GOLDENE MEDINE*, THE 'GOLDEN LAND', THEY MEANT THE USA. IT WAS A PLACE OF OPPORTUNITY, LARGELY FREE OF 'OLD EUROPE'S' PREJUDICES.

The Anglo-Jewish author Israel Zangwill famously called America a 'melting pot' in which former identities would dissolve and people would emerge as equal citizens. Many Jews thought America signalled the end of 'Diaspora persecution', even if it was not exactly the biblical 'promised land'. Jewish women were important to American social activism, and included such figures as Rebecca Gratz, educator of poor women, and Lillian Wald, a healthcare pioneer.

SETTLING IN THE USA

The first wave of Jews to the USA were Sephardim from Brazil and Holland; the second wave were educated German Jews; and the third and largest were Yiddish-speaking eastern Europeans, originally fleeing the 1881 pogroms in Russia.

Below *An American gold prospector wearing Levi's jeans.*

Uncomfortable with indigenous religious liberality, some 'third wave' traditional Jews created an Orthodox Congregation Union in 1898. Many others joined the Reform and Conservative movements, which seemed closer to the American ethos, while others clung to Yiddish culture even if they lost their faith.

Between 1800 and 1860 America's Jewish population had leapt to more than 100,000. This growth inspired the creation in 1843 of the *B'nai Brit*, or 'Sons of the Covenant', America's first nationwide Jewish secular organization.

JEWS IN THE WILD WEST AND IN CONGRESS

The great 19th-century move west attracted entrepreneurs such as the Gratz family of Philadelphia, who developed the new terrain with their expertise in banking, insurance and railroads. Likewise, the German-born Levi Strauss (1829–1902) found a ready market for his invention, hardy denim jeans, among the prospectors in the 1848 California Gold Rush.

Meanwhile, in New York, Mordecai Manuel Noah (1785–1851), an eccentric playwright and newspaper editor, led the Democrat Party's political machine. Noah fought to abolish slavery, and also campaigned for a Jewish homeland on an island in the Niagara.

Jews were also represented in the Deep South: as early as the 1670s Sephardim had settled in Charleston, South Carolina. Florida railroad pioneer David Levy Yulee (1810–66) became the first Jew elected to the Senate in 1845. Jewish senator Judah Benjamin (1811–84) became war secretary in the southern Confederate cabinet.

Above *Emma Lazarus was an American Jew born in New York City. Her poem 'Colossus' welcomed immigrants at Ellis Island with: 'Give me your huddled masses yearning to be free.'*

REFORM AND CONSERVATIVE JUDAISM

The Bohemian-born rabbi and organizational dynamo Isaac Mayer Wise (1819–1900) effectively founded modern American Reform Judaism in Cincinnati after 1854. Samuel Hirsch (1815–89) from the Rhineland then brought a more philosophical perspective as president of the Conference of American Reform Rabbis in 1869. The flagship Hebrew Union College, created in 1875, soon signalled that American Reform was set on a path distinct from its European roots.

Others balked at Hirsch's radicalism, yet found Orthodoxy too constraining. In 1886 they set up New York's Jewish Theological Seminary to promote their values. Called Conservative Jews and later inspired by the scholastic Rabbi Solomon Schechter, they founded synagogues after 1913 and by the mid-20th century they formed America's largest Jewish denomination.

DIASPORAS OF THE SOUTHERN HEMISPHERE

FOR CENTURIES, JEWISH HISTORY TOOK PLACE EXCLUSIVELY NORTH OF THE EQUATOR. WITH 18TH- AND 19TH-CENTURY COLONIAL EXPANSION, NEW COMMUNITIES AROSE IN THE SOUTHERN HEMISPHERE.

Many Jews travelled to the Southern Hemisphere after the 1881 Russian Pogroms. Few, if any, Jews lived there already and it was hard to lead a traditional Jewish life. Immigrants exploited economic opportunities in frontier societies that could ill-afford the old prejudices of Europe and soon established new Jewish communities, schools and institutions.

SOUTH AFRICA

There were few practising Jews among the Dutch who settled in South Africa in 1652. More arrived in the 1820s after Britain took over the Cape Colony, and larger numbers followed with the diamond and gold-mining boom in the late 1800s.

Initially, most Jews came from Britain. As travelling salesmen they connected remote farmsteads with larger towns; a bilingual Yiddish–Zulu lexicon helped them trade with Black Africans. A few became the wealthy heads of mining finance houses, like Alfred Beit, Barney Barnato, Lionel Phillips and Solly Joel.

Many more Ashkenazim came from Lithuania and Latvia after 1881, and Jews made up 23 per cent of all immigrants to the Cape 1885–1915. These 'Litvaks' tended to gravitate to Cape Town and Johannesburg where, considerably poorer than the gold magnates, they worked as tailors or small shopkeepers. They encouraged their children to train for the professions, and set up their own Board of Deputies in 1904.

AUSTRALIA

The first Jews in Australia arrived as convicts in 1788. Their descendants bought a burial plot in 1820; in 1832 they formed a congregation under Aaron Levi; and in 1844 built their first synagogue in Sydney. Tasmania was probably the next place of settlement. Gold rushes attracted immigrants to Melbourne in the 1850s, and Perth in the 1890s. One prominent Australian-born Jew of the period was the architect Nahum Barnet, who built synagogues, department stores, factories and theatres.

Above *Great Synagogue and Jewish Museum in Cape Town, South Africa.*

SOUTH AMERICA

Portuguese traders and smugglers in the Rio de la Plata most likely included a few Sephardim, but French Jews established the first true Argentinean community after the country won independence in 1810. A large post-1881 influx of 'Rusos' boosted the Ashkenazi proportion of the population to 80 per cent, while others came from Morocco.

Baron Maurice de Hirsch considered Argentina an alternative Zion and bought farmland in Santa Fe and Entre Rios provinces. Soon Yiddish-speaking gauchos were herding cattle. Over time, their *communas* (small towns) began resembling east European *shtetls*. By 1920, most of Argentina's 150,000 Jews lived in larger cities.

A liberal 1824 constitution and a booming trade in rubber made Brazil the second largest Latin American destination for Jews. Mexican Emperor Maximilian I encouraged German Jews to come to his kingdom, and Sephardi Jews fleeing an ailing Ottoman empire made new homes on the continent.

Left *Consecrated in 1877, Mikve Israel Synagogue in Melbourne symbolizes Jewish roots planted in Australia.*

JEWS OF THE LATE OTTOMAN EMPIRE

WITHIN A SLOWLY STAGNATING EMPIRE, SALONIKA REMAINED A MAGNET FOR JEWISH IMMIGRATION, A HUB OF SCHOLARSHIP AND INNOVATION, AND A VIBRANT MOSAIC OF CULTURES AND CLASSES.

In 1683 the Turks alarmed Europe when they laid siege to Vienna. Yet two months later they were repelled, after which the Ottoman empire began its gradual decline. Constantinople's reluctance to industrialize hampered its economy, and from the 16th century European trade vessels bypassed the Ottomans, sailing direct to India and the Americas. By the 19th century, Western officials mocked Turkey as 'The Sick Man of Europe'.

DECLINE AND SURVIVAL

Wars deprived Turkey of parts of Greece, Hungary and the Black Sea, and the Congress of Berlin of 1878 further chipped away at the empire. Despite this, belated reforms enhanced civil rights and five Jews sat in the Ottoman parliament by 1887. Some Jews benefited from laws, first introduced in 1536, that privileged foreign traders. Yet the overall effect was negative; Jews in Egypt, for example, felt relieved when the former Ottoman province came under British protection in 1882. The Young Turk revolt of 1908 briefly offered new hope, until in 1914 the empire erred fatally in backing Germany in World War I.

SALONIKA

Ruled by Turks since 1430, Salonika in north-eastern Greece – today, Thessaloniki – became the mainstay of Sephardi Jewry. New immigrants enriched the community: Hungarians after 1376, Bavarian Ashkenazim in 1470, Jews from Venice and Sicily, and most of all Spanish exiles and Maranos, especially after 1492. By 1514 Jews formed more than half the population, and Salonika, an early hub of Hebrew printing, was dubbed the 'Mother of Israel'

Jews were pivotal to the wool and silk trades. After 1515 they provided the Ottoman army with uniforms. Many also worked as miners, jewellers, dockers and fishermen. In 1680 the Jewish communities united to elect one assembly. By 1900 they made up 80,000 of the city's 173,000 inhabitants. Sephardim dominated: local dishes and songs bore an Iberian flavour; gentile Greeks, Armenians and Turks came to speak their Ladino language; and the busy port closed for the Sabbath.

Jewish colleges taught astronomy, medicine and sciences from the 1500s. An Alliance Israélite school in 1874 encouraged liberal attitudes. More Jews became lawyers, doctors and bankers, and Emmanuel Carasso and Marcel Samuel Cohen were prominent Young Turk leaders. During 1880–1910 secular Ladino theatres and newspapers flourished, along with socialist and Zionist clubs. But Orthodox stalwarts often clashed with wealthy families who favoured the French language and Western values.

Jews began leaving Salonika after Greece captured the city in 1912, and fire destroyed homes and businesses in 1917. In 1943 the Nazis deported 95 per cent of those who stayed, up to 56,000 people – almost all perished in Auschwitz.

Today descendants of Ottoman Jews live on in Istanbul, New York, London, Paris and Israel.

Above *Jewish porter in the Greek city of Salonika, late Ottoman period.*

Left *Dolmabahçe Palace, home to the last six Ottoman sultans, in Constantinople (now Istanbul).*

POLITICAL ZIONISM

ONE OF MANY IDEOLOGIES THAT TRIED TO ANSWER JEWISH YEARNINGS, POLITICAL ZIONISM GRAFTED MODERN NATIONALIST IDEAS ON TO THE ANCIENT CONNECTION OF JEWS TO THE LAND OF ISRAEL.

Coined by the publicist Nathan Birnbaum, the expression 'Zionism' derives from Mount Zion, which adjoins the Old City of Jerusalem. At its simplest, Zionism acknowledges Jewry's attachment to the Land of Israel that broadly covers present-day Israel and the West Bank of the River Jordan. Some draw a distinction between spiritual Zionism, which has underpinned the Jewish religion since the Babylonian Exile, and political Zionism, which crystallized in Europe in the late 19th century.

TOWARDS A JEWISH NATIONALISM

Increasingly, followers of the *Haskalah* (Jewish Enlightenment) defined themselves as a nation, not a religion. And as every nation should have a land, so should the Jews, they concluded. The German Jewish philosopher Moses Hess (1812–75) exemplified this ideology. He wrote in his 1862 book *Rome and Jerusalem* that Jewish national feeling was unquenchable and could only be expressed by physically returning to Palestine. If necessary, Jews should sacrifice emancipation in the Diaspora for this cause.

ODESSA AND THE 1881 POGROMS

Few noticed Hess's book until two men from Odessa, Leon Pinsker (1821–91) and Ahad Ha-Am (1856–1927), revived its ideas. Odessa on the Black Sea was one-third Jewish and housed some 150,000 of the most secular, educated and assimilated Jews in Russia. The pogroms of 1881 shattered dreams of integration and prompted Pinsker to write *Auto-emancipation*, in which he declared: 'For the living, the Jew is a dead man; for the natives, an alien and a vagrant; for the patriot, a man without a country; for all classes, a hated rival'. Jews would only enjoy respect when they liberated themselves, he said.

Pinsker headed *Hovevei Tzion* (Lovers of Zion), which founded Rishon le-Tzion as the first Zionist settlement in Palestine in 1882. Baron Edmond de Rothschild began to help, and Russian Jewish students, called *Bilu*, started the first *aliyah*, or 'ascent', or wave of immigration.

THEODOR HERZL AND THE DIPLOMATIC PATH

Hovevei set up an Odessa Committee in 1890 to plan Jewish farming in Palestine, but lacked political direction. Ultimately it was Theodor Herzl (1860–1904) who filled that need. Earlier he had mused about 'solving the Jewish problem' through mass conversion. While reporting from Paris in 1895, he heard crowds baying for Jewish blood at the court

Above *Confident, elegant, romantic yet controversial, Theodor Herzl galvanized the nascent Zionist movement. The text above the picture bears his famous words, 'If you will it, it is no fairytale.'*

Left *'In Basel I founded the Jewish State', wrote Herzl in 1897. Here he is with delegates at the fifth Zionist conference in the same Swiss city.*

martial of Alfred Dreyfus, a Jewish colonel falsely accused of treason. Now convinced that even cultured France was irredeemably anti-Semitic, he wrote his monograph *Judenstaat*, or 'Jewish State', in 1896, which argued that the Jewish Question was national in essence, not individual; Jews could only enjoy true freedom if they governed themselves, preferably on 'ancestral soil'.

Judenstaat became Zionism's manifesto and Herzl, a man of rare panache and regal bearing, gained messianic status among some east European *Ostjuden*. Most Jews, however, were less enthusiastic. Most Jewish philanthropists rebuffed him as a dangerous dreamer.

THE BASEL CONFERENCE

In 1897 Herzl and his colleague Max Nordau convened the first Zionist conference in Basel, Switzerland. There they created an organization and a 'national fund'. Two trends quickly emerged within Zionism. General or political Zionism followed Herzl's diplomatic path, while Ahad Ha-Am persisted with cultural Zionism. Aaron David Gordon (1856–1922) later led practical Zionists who saw settlement in Palestine as a way to create a 'new Jew' through the dignity of labour.

Herzl wrote in his diary after the conference, 'In Basel I founded the Jewish State... Maybe in five years, certainly in fifty, everyone will realize it'. At the time it seemed an extraordinary prediction; Zionism was only one of dozens of Jewish ideologies.

NEW TRENDS

Gradually a third stream, known as Labour Zionism, became dominant in the early 20th century. It consisted of divergent elements, including a romantic back-to-nature trend called Po'ale Tza'ir (Young Worker) and a more Marxist grouping, Po'ale Zion (Worker of Zion).

Above *Jewish men and women pray at the Western Wall, Jerusalem, c.1905.*

A fourth stream emerged, Religious Zionism, which opposed both the secularists who dominated the Zionist movement and the anti-Zionists who made up most observant Jews. In 1902 this group held its first conference in Vilna under its leader, Rabbi Yizhak Reines. Finally Nordau and others who came to despair of gradualism advocated what they called Catastrophic Zionism.

THE UGANDA OPTION

Herzl envisaged a Jewish-ruled yet pluralist Palestine, a bourgeois European-style utopian paradise in the Levant, as seen in his 1902 novel *Altneuland* (Old-New Land). Even fellow Zionists mocked its naïve dream of Jerusalem as a capital of world peace, or its belief that Arabs would welcome Jewish settlement.

When Britain's foreign office offered Herzl a tract of land in Uganda/Kenya, he agreed immediately. The seventh congress in 1905, however, rejected the Uganda Option, by which time Herzl had died of exhaustion in July 1904.

Ultimately, Zionism's fate depended on external factors, the collapse of Ottoman rule and Britain's acquisition of Palestine. The challenge was reconciling the national feelings of Jews and the land's indigenous Arab majority. As early as 1891 Ahad Ha-Am warned in *The Truth from Palestine* that it was not, as some imagined, 'a land without people'. The Marxist Zionist, Ber Borochov, dreamt of Jewish and Arab workers uniting; however, Ha-Am noted that if any Arab felt oppressed by Jews, 'rage will stay alive in his heart'.

JERUSALEM – BEYOND THE CITY WALLS

During 1537–42 the Ottoman Sultan Suleiman built Jerusalem's majestic walls and eight gates, which still define the Old City today. Within those walls are Muslim, Christian, Jewish and Armenian quarters. At the centre stands the Temple Mount, or Haram al-Sharif, site of two Muslim mosques and believed by Jews to be the location of the twice-destroyed Temple. Every day religious Jews pray to God for 'remembrance of Jerusalem Your Holy City' and the 'return of the Divine Presence to Zion'.

After 1700 Polish and Moroccan Jews began filling up the Jewish quarter; soon the Old City became overcrowded. In 1860 Sir Moses Montefiore, an English Sephardi benefactor, won approval for Jewish suburbs to be built outside the walls, the first being Mishkenot Sha'ananim. Soon Muslim and Christian Arabs built their own neighbourhoods, though by the 1870s Jews probably constituted the majority of the city's population.

Early Zionists felt ambivalent about the city, because it was a centre for religious Jews who depended on charity and rejected their secular venture. To Zionists, these long-established Jews paradoxically represented the worst aspects of 'non-productive' Diaspora life.

CHAPTER 4

WORLD WARS AND THE HOLOCAUST

More than 20 million people died in World War I between 1914 and 1918, and when fighting ceased, both Jews and Gentiles understandably longed for peace. The interwar years saw individual Jews flower in the arts, sciences and politics as never before. The more radical welcomed Russia's 1917 Communist Revolution, especially when it outlawed anti-Semitism and abolished the pernicious Pale of Settlement.

Yet many ordinary Germans believed that Jews had betrayed the fatherland. Increasingly they backed Adolf Hitler's ultra-nationalist Nazi Party, which vowed to exterminate 'non-Aryans' and, during World War II (1939–45), almost succeeded. In 1942 the Nazis began the industrialized murder of 6 million Jews, including 1.5 million children. Called the Holocaust, or Shoah in Hebrew, this systematic genocide virtually destroyed 1,500 years of European Jewish civilization. Recalled in monuments, museums, novels and films, it remains a benchmark for mankind's capacity for evil.

Opposite *Shoes at the former Nazi extermination camp of Auschwitz, Poland. Up to 1.5 million men, women and children, mostly Jews, were murdered there in 1942–4. The Holocaust marked a nadir in human history and nearly wiped out Jewish life in Europe.*

Above *Prisoners are led through the gates of Theresienstadt concentration camp, c. 1942. Inscribed above the entrance is 'Arbeit macht frei' ('Work will set you free') – a supremely cynical motto.*

EUROPE AT WAR

SOME 1.5 MILLION JEWS SERVED AS SOLDIERS IN WORLD WAR I, THE CONFLICT THAT TRANSFORMED EUROPE AND INDIRECTLY LED BRITAIN TO PROMISE JEWS A 'NATIONAL HOME' IN PALESTINE.

Above A.J. Balfour, British Foreign Secretary, whose 1917 Declaration pledged a national homeland for Jews.

Even before World War I broke out, life was turbulent for Jews in eastern Europe. Violence against Jews during Russia's 1905 uprisings led to 154,000 Jews moving to the USA during 1905–6. Smaller numbers went to France and Britain. In 1904–14 40,000 mainly socialist, east European Jews moved to Palestine. This Aliyah, or 'ascent', laid foundations for the Zionist labour movement, the Hebrew press and the *kvutzot*, or 'communal farming settlements'.

THE PATH OF WAR

Austria's Archduke Franz Ferdinand's assassination in Sarajevo, Bosnia, on 28 June 1914 led to the most murderous war to date. By August, a series of alliances had been activated, with the Entente Powers – Britain, France, Serbia and imperial Russia – fighting the Central Powers of Germany and Austria-Hungary, Ottoman Turkey and Bulgaria.

Hopes of swift victory faded as trench warfare came to western Europe. The technology that enabled mass production of electric lighting, telephones, radio, railway networks and cars now drove the world's first truly industrial war. The conflict was fought on land, sea and air and across six separate fronts. Over four years, 65 million troops were mobilized, 8.5 million killed, 21.2 million wounded, and 7.8 million taken prisoner or listed as missing in action. Another 13 million non-combatants probably died through hostilities and disease.

SOLDIERS ON ALL SIDES

All leading German Jewish intellectuals – except Albert Einstein – signed a petition supporting German war aims. Some 100,000 Jews fought for Germany, proportionately more than any other ethnic, religious or political group, and about 12,000 died in battle. Jews from European colonies also enlisted, and Algerian Jewish soldiers were particularly noted for their courage in battle.

Jews in England and America felt uncomfortable joining any alliance with Russia's anti-Jewish Tsar. Despite this, 50,000 Jews served in the British forces, of whom five won the Victoria Cross and 50 the Distinguished Service Order. Many worked in labour corps in Middlesex, Egypt and the French trenches, while a few joined the Zion Mule Corps.

The Russian Imperial Army fielded 400,000–650,000 Jewish troops, more than any other nation; possibly 100,000 Russian Jews died in the conflict. Early in the war, Russian officials expelled Jews from the Pale of Settlement.

After 1915 some 40 per cent of Russian Jews came under German and Austrian military rule. Most welcomed their better treatment yet regretted being cut off from brethren to the east. By 1917, 3.4 million Jews remained under Russian rule, 700,000 of them beyond the Pale.

Left Europe in 1914, showing the disposition of forces before a war that was to claim 21 million lives.

America's entry into the war in April 1917 ultimately tipped the balance and resulted in an Entente victory, but not before a late eastern push by Germany encouraged war-weary Russians to force their Tsar to abdicate in February 1917.

A WAR TO END ALL WARS?

Europe was transformed when the Great War ended with the armistice of 11 November 1918. Gone were the Ottoman and Austro-Hungarian empires and the German Second Reich. New states including Czechoslovakia and Yugoslavia emerged, and Poland was independent for the first time in 100 years.

The war had turned America into a global superpower, and US President Woodrow Wilson promoted a League of Nations to prevent future conflict. Yet the same Versailles Treaty that created the League in 1920 so harshly punished Germany, it virtually guaranteed another war.

BALFOUR'S DECLARATION

Barely noticed amid the clamour of war was a letter that Britain's foreign secretary James Balfour wrote to Lord Rothschild on 2 November 1917. In it, Balfour stated that his government 'views with favour the establishment of a Jewish national home in Palestine'. The Balfour Declaration, brief and unspecific though it was, marked the first Great Power approval for a Jewish political entity on 'ancestral soil' in 1,900 years. The letter crowned years of diplomacy by Chaim Weizmann and Nahum Sokolow of the World Zionist Organization. Weizmann's technical assistance to Britain's war effort also helped clinch the agreement. Yet most European Jews remained sceptical about Zionism. And five days after Balfour signed his letter, Russian Bolshevik militants launched a Marxist revolution that raised Jewish hopes for a more promising solution.

THE WAR IN PALESTINE

Above *Pte Nathaniel Friedlander, a Jewish barber from London, after signing up to fight with the Army Service Corps, 1915.*

Although Zionists and many Jews backed Turkey and Germany over the Allies, dissidents saw an opportunity to plan a future Jewish state by backing the Allied powers. In late 1914, Vladimir Jabotinsky and Joseph Trumpeldor persuaded Britain to create the Zion Mule Corps, a Jewish transportation unit. This disbanded in 1915, but inspired the 1917 establishment of the Jewish Legion.

Palestinian Jewish spies were siphoning information to Britain on Turkish movements, as French troops were mobilizing in Syria and Lebanon. Jews and Arabs, French and British, were all fighting against a Turkish enemy.

Eventually, on 11 December 1917, Britain's General Allenby entered Jerusalem and accepted a Turkish surrender. In 1918 a Jewish Legion battalion led a British crossing of the Jordan River into Palestine. So ended 500 years of Ottoman rule over the Holy Land. Allied and Arab forces took Damascus, Beirut and Aleppo by the end of 1918.

Below *Jewish soldiers from Austria, Hungary and Poland at prayer, military camp, 1914, first year of World War I. By the Jewish painter O. Ehrenfreund.*

Below *United in death: German soldiers, one Jewish, one Christian, buried side by side at a French war cemetery.*

Jews and the Bolshevik Revolution

Russia, home to half the world's Jews, was still a semi-feudalistic state in the early 1900s. The 1917 revolutions marked a dramatic shift, but the Jews were later to suffer under Communist rule too.

By the 1900s, Russia's Jewish socialists were deeply divided. Many belonged to the leading Marxist Social Democratic Party, which was itself split between moderate Mensheviks and radical Bolsheviks. For their part, Socialist Zionists, called Po'ale Zion, or 'Workers of Zion', threw their weight behind the 1917 October revolution.

REVOLUTION, WAR, AND THE END OF THE PALE

The Bund, a Jewish Labour Union, had been founded in 1897 to achieve equality for Jews in the Russian empire. Bundists also led the 1905 revolutionary uprisings, which resulted in limited political reforms.

Below *Born to a Jewish family, Leon Trotsky embraced Marxism and helped lead the 1917 Russian Revolution.*

However, a backlash led to 500 Odessa Jews being killed in a single day, and Marxists boycotted elections to a Duma (parliament) that was soon dissolved anyway.

Russia entered World War I on 1 August 1914, woefully unprepared and allied with Britain and France against the Central Powers. Fighting largely took place in areas where Russian Jews lived. Tsar Nicholas II took personal command of forces in September 1915, but by 1917 crippling losses caused them to reject rule by the 'Little Father of the People'. In March 1917 Nicholas was forced to abdicate. Russia's new provisional government abolished the Pale of Settlement.

STORMING THE KREMLIN

Exiled Bolsheviks stole back into Russia on board a 'sealed train' from Switzerland in April 1917, led by Vladimir Lenin (1870–1924) and his chief aide, Grigory Zinoviev (born Hirsch Apfelbaum, a Jew by origin, 1883–1936). Defying orthodox Marxist qualms, in October Lenin seized St Petersburg and Moscow and within weeks the centralized empire fell to his Bolshevik cadres.

Their astonishing success would have been impossible without the organizational skills of Leon Trotsky, born in 1878 as Lev Davidovich Bronstein. His father was an illiterate Jewish Ukrainian farmer.

In January 1918 the Bolsheviks banned other parties and declared a Soviet Republic. Mensheviks were tolerated as allies temporarily, but were outlawed in 1921.

Above *The future is red – 1924 propaganda poster of Bolshevik revolutionary leader Vladimir Lenin.*

RUINOUS CIVIL WAR

In March 1918 Trotsky signed the controversial Brest–Litovsk peace treaty with Germany, which pulled Russia out of the war and ceded Poland and the Baltic States. By now a vicious civil war had erupted between Bolsheviks, or Reds, and Counter-revolutionaries, or Whites, a motley coalition of monarchists, liberals and local nationalists backed by Allied powers. This conflict raged for four years and included rightist pogroms that killed more than 70,000 Jewish civilians. More Jews now backed the Bolsheviks, even though some renegade Red troops had also ransacked *shtetls* (Jewish villages).

JEWS IN NEW RUSSIA

Dozens of Jewish-origin Bolsheviks now wielded power over the largest nation on earth. Lenin was himself part-Jewish, and four of his politburo's seven members had Jewish blood, including Zinoviev, Trotsky and Lev Kamenev. Another Jew, Adolph Joffe, chaired the St Petersburg Military Revolutionary

Committee that overthrew the provisional government. Jews even ran their own Communist party cell, the *Yevsektsiya*.

Soviet rule brought changes for ordinary Jews, initially for the better. In July 1918 the Communists passed a decree 'recognizing the equality of all citizens, irrespective of race or nationality', and Lenin unequivocally proclaimed in 1919: 'Shame on accursed Tsarism which tortured and persecuted the Jews'.

With the Pale gone, Jews could, in theory, live anywhere. Jews formed soviets (workers' councils). The Kremlin decided to transform Jewish pedlars and petty artisans into farmers, to integrate Jews into society and eradicate anti-Semitism. By contrast with trends everywhere else, Jews left cities for the countryside. By 1930 some 230,000 Jews were working on farming communes in Belarus, Crimea and Ukraine.

FREEDOM EXTINGUISHED

Soon Communism revealed a darker side. The authorities penalized small Jewish shopkeepers and artisans as 'bourgeois elements' and closed churches, mosques and synagogues alike after 1921. The Evseksia summarily crushed all other Jewish organizations and ran 'community trials' against 'backward and chauvinistic' Jewish religious practices, before it, too, was disbanded in 1930. As the Russian-born Zionist Chaim Weizmann noted, the revolutionaries 'could not understand why a Russian Jew should want to be anything but a Russian'.

Joseph Stalin gradually monopolized power after Lenin's death in 1924 by sidelining, arresting or expelling rivals, notably including Kamenev, Zinoviev and Trotsky. Agricultural collectivization led to rampant famine, especially in Ukraine, which killed millions. Show trials after 1934 purged most old Bolsheviks, including thousands of Jewish origin, and former tolerance of Yiddish cultural autonomy gave way to enforced assimilation by the late 1930s. But at least the physical survival of Jews was not threatened by communist rule, as it was in Nazi Germany and fascist Europe.

Left Capturing the excitement of a new era, this Bolshevik poster calls on foreign workers to join the Revolution.

Above Soviet Jewish collective farmer Michael Gefen and wife Sheina tend their homestead in Birobidzhan, 1935.

BIROBIDZHAN

The USSR's politburo wanted to assign a homeland to each nationality, including the Jews. Communism opposed Zionism so Palestine was no option. In 1928, the USSR set up the town of Birobidzhan at the end of the Trans-Siberian railway, to be the capital of a Jewish Autonomous Region, Yevreskaya. Yiddish and Russian were its official languages, and Jews were encouraged to farm and work in factories. However conditions were poor, Hebrew and religious instruction were outlawed, and, though the Kremlin boasted 150,000 Jews would live in Birobidzhan by 1937, few actually did. Only 25,000 were there in 1974, and 4,000 in 2008.

Birobidzhan experienced a slight revival after the fall of the Soviet Union, but it never fulfilled its aim of becoming a Marxist 'alternative Zion'.

THE INTERWAR YEARS

AFTER THE DEVASTATION OF WORLD WAR I, THE LEAGUE OF NATIONS WAS ESTABLISHED IN 1919 TO GUARANTEE GLOBAL PEACE. IN FACT THE RESULTANT TREATIES CREATED MORE PROBLEMS THAN THEY SOLVED.

Above Socialist firebrand Rosa Luxemburg, murdered in 1919 after an abortive coup in Berlin.

From a Jewish perspective the interwar years presented a portrait of contrasts. On the one hand individual Jews thrived as never before; on the other, hatred against Jews mounted. And after Nazis took over Germany in 1933, both individuals and communities across Europe faced the real threat of annihilation.

JEWISH DELEGATES TO VERSAILES

The Paris peace talks of 1919 aimed to establish a new world order where all peoples had a voice. In this spirit, Jews sent a deputation called the Comité Des Delegations Juives, claiming the support of 12 million people worldwide. Led by US lawyer Louis Marshall and Russian Zionist Leo Motzkin, the Comité demanded protection for Jews as a nationality, albeit a stateless one. In the event Jews were acknowledged as a semi-autonomous minority.

The Versailles Treaty of 1919 recognized a host of new states, including Poland, Lithuania, Czechoslovakia and Yugoslavia. Austria was stripped down to its core area, Hungary won its independence and Germany's Weimar Republic had to cede economically valuable land to neighbours.

Left The League of Nations was the brainchild of President Woodrow Wilson, seen here reassuring a nervous USA.

Versailles was hardly ideal for Jews. Before 1914 they had lived with other minorities in ramshackle empires but now they felt exposed. Versailles compelled eastern European states to sign minority rights treaties following Comité advice, though Poland, Hungary and Romania subverted this requirement by targeted taxation, or laws to improve trade and sanitation. Furthermore, rifts between pro- and anti-Zionists undermined the Comité and similar bodies such as the Jewish Agency and World Jewish Congress.

THE STAB IN THE BACK

Conspiracy theorists in Germany's ultra-nationalist *Freikorps* group spread the myth that Jews had stabbed Germany in the back by forcing the fatherland to surrender just when it was about to win the war. Meanwhile, rightists in Russia and beyond blamed the Jews for the 1917 revolution and subsequent ruinous civil war; even though most ordinary Jews were apolitical residents of the Pale, remote from events in Moscow and Petrograd.

JEWISH REVOLUTIONARIES IN GERMANY

In November 1918, as Germany sank to military defeat, Jewish socialist Kurt Eisner overthrew the Bavarian monarchy and founded a 'people's republic'. When he was assassinated the next February, other Jewish revolutionaries, Ernst Toller, Gustav Landauer and Eugene Leviné, established a short-lived Soviet republic there in imitation of the Bolsheviks in Russia.

The best-known Jewish radical of all was the Polish-born Rosa Luxemburg (1871–1919). Formerly the co-founder of the Lithuanian Social-Democratic Party, she moved to Germany in 1898 and soon rejected the parliamentary approach. Her inveterate foe was another Jew, the revisionist Marxist Eduard Bernstein, a Social-Democrat leader and Reichstag member during 1902–18 and 1920–28. Luxemburg took a bolder stance: a fiery critic of imperialism, nationalism and even Bolshevik 'bureaucracy', she co-founded the Spartacist League in 1914, which unlike mainstream socialists opposed the war and supported spontaneous uprising by the masses. Army officers murdered her in January 1919 after a failed Spartacist coup attempt in Berlin. The leftist Jewish historian Isaac Deutscher later called her assassination 'the first triumph of Nazi Germany'.

Neither Rosa Luxemburg nor most Marxists of Jewish origin cared much for Judaism. Nor did most German Jews support their views.

Above The old world meets the new? Erich Lessing's painting shows a Polish Jewish soldier reading a newspaper to his countrymen, 1920.

None the less, the prominence of Jewish revolutionary leaders allowed rightists to tar the whole community with the 'radical' brush.

JEWISH LIFE IN POLAND

Having been missing from the map of Europe since the partition of 1816, Poland was reborn as an independent nation under Marshal Joseph Pilsudski on 11 November 1918. Thousands of Jewish shopkeepers, professionals and petty capitalists voted with their feet and moved there. By 1924, Poland had nearly 3 million Jews, more than 10 per cent of its population. Jews made up about a quarter of all schoolchildren and university students. Polish Jews generally felt well disposed towards Pilsudski, who named himself dictator in May 1926 and implemented the terms of the 1919 Minorities Protection Treaty.

Poland's Jewish urban dwellers increasingly spoke Polish and revelled in a buoyant national culture, whereas poorer rural Jews stuck to Yiddish and cherished traditional ways. Jewish political parties now entered the *Sejm*, or 'Polish parliament', initially as a national council in co-operation with other minorities. After 1928 some Jewish parties joined the government list – a new phenomenon that split Jewish votes and eroded the community's independence.

Leftist and Zionist Jewish groups competed with each other more productively in Poland and Lithuania by building networks of secular schools. Instruction was either in Yiddish or Hebrew and the development marked a breach with previous tradition.

THE MARCH OF FASCISM

All Europe suffered from the Wall Street stock market crash of 1929, and as unemployment and inflation ran rampant, fascism grew in Austria, Hungary and Poland. Fanatics began to follow the model set by Benito Mussolini's Italian Fascists who took power in October 1922. Fascism venerated the state, rejected capitalism and Marxism in equal measure, and marked, in Mussolini's words, the clear, final and categorical antithesis of democracy, plutocracy, freemasonry and the principles of 1789. Every state in Europe was under democratic government in the 1920s; by 1940 only four democracies had survived.

At first fascism was not explicitly anti-Semitic, but it provided an environment within which racism could thrive. Ultimately Nazism, the Germanic variant of fascism, transformed racism into a commanding ideology, dragged the world into a second world war, and all but destroyed the Jews of Europe.

AMERICA – PROGRESS AND PITFALLS

Above Ku Klux Klan devotees, Long Island, New York State, 1930.

World War I helped establish American centrality in world affairs, and Jews became an integral part of US society. The first Jewish state governor, Moses Alexander of Idaho, was elected in 1915; Louis Brandeis became the first Jew in the US Supreme Court in 1916; and in 1917 Jews made up 5.7% of the US Army, greater than their 3.25% representation in the population.

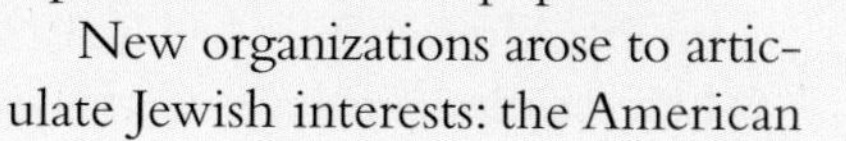

New organizations arose to articulate Jewish interests: the American Jewish Joint Distribution Committee in 1914, and the American Jewish Congress (AJC) in 1918. Reconstituted under Steven Wise in 1924, in 1936 the AJC propelled the creation of a World Jewish Congress. Brandeis, Wise and Felix Frankfurter were powerful advocates for Zionism; and immigrants benefited American science, industry and popular culture.

However, an influx of comparatively unskilled workers strained the economy and led to new quotas. The 1924 Immigration Act capped entrants by area of origin to 2% of any donor country's community present in the USA in 1880, thus targeting Asians and eastern and southern Europeans, including Jews. Latent anti-Semitism came to the fore, with car tycoon Henry Ford disseminating the Protocols of Zion, and others backing the 1924 act on grounds of racial hygiene. Following the 1929 slump, the racist Ku Klux Klan added Jews as another enemy of America, and anti-Semitic organizations, some sponsored by Germany after 1933, lambasted President Roosevelt's New Deal as a Jew Deal. In 1938 the Catholic radio priest Charles Coughlin launched a propaganda campaign against Jews. Despite this, when war erupted in September 1939 most Americans united against Nazi aggression.

WORLD WAR II BEGINS

THE GERMAN DRIVE FOR *LEBENSRAUM*, OR 'LIVING SPACE', ULTIMATELY SPARKED WORLD WAR II. AS MORE COUNTRIES WERE CONQUERED, SO MILLIONS OF JEWS FELL PREY TO LETHAL NAZI LEGISLATION.

At first, the Nazis only coveted lands lost in 1918. They acquired the port of Danzig after 1933, and overran the coal-rich Saar region in 1935 and German Upper Silesia in 1937. Facing mere rebukes from France, Britain and the League of Nations, Hitler felt emboldened to fuse his native Austria with Germany, although the 1919 Versailles Treaty had expressly forbidden this.

On 12 March 1938, German troops invaded Austria and arrested 70,000 leading Jews, Communists and Social Democrats. Hitler then declared Germany and Austria one, entered Vienna and Linz in triumph and applied racial legislation against Austria's 190,000 Jews, about three-quarters of whom lived in Vienna.

***Below** Internees building Dachau, Germany's first concentration camp, under the watch of an SS guard, 1933.*

EVIAN CONFERENCE

By 1938, about 150,000, or nearly one-third, of Germany's 500,000 Jews had emigrated; and more Jews left from occupied Danzig, Saar, Silesia and Sudetenland. In July 1938, US President Franklin Roosevelt convened a nine-day conference to address the refugee issue at Evian-les-Bains, France. All told, some 811,000 Jews managed to find new homes abroad during the period 1933–43: 190,000 went to America, 120,000 to Palestine and 65,000 to England.

NIGHT OF BROKEN GLASS

The true nadir arrived with the cross-continental pogrom against Jews in Germany and Austria on 9–10 November 1938. Dubbed *Kristallnacht*, or 'Night of Broken Glass', this onslaught saw 1,000 synagogues destroyed, dozens of Jews killed, businesses looted, properties resold at forced auctions and wealth stolen by Nazi thugs. Five days later Germany closed all public schools to Jewish children.

***Above** Kristallnacht, November 1938, when looters ransacked Jewish shops with the connivance of the regime.*

Kristallnacht shocked the world and hastened the likelihood of war. Responding to pleas from British Jews, Britain agreed to rescue 10,000 unaccompanied Jewish children in what was called the *Kindertransport*. A similar initiative in America was sadly blocked at Congressional Committee stage.

THE FALL OF POLAND

Adolf Hitler's final gamble was his non-aggression pact with the Soviet Union of 24 August 1939, which effectively neutralized Germany's 'eastern front'. The way was now clear for Hitler to invade Poland on 1 September 1939. Some 20,000 Jews died in the initial incursion, and bombing destroyed up to 95 per cent of Jewish homes in 120 centres. Poland was divided into two zones, German in the west (with 2.1 million Jews) and Russian in the east (with 1.37 million Jews). From

Above *Lithuanian soldier marching a group of Jews to forced labour in Nazi-occupied eastern Europe.*

October 1939 Nazis began corralling Jews into urban ghettos, with the Warsaw Ghetto holding 380,000 and Lodz, 160,000. Conditions were appalling: Jews, nearly a third of Warsaw's population, occupied just 2.4 per cent of the city's area. Thousands died of disease and starvation as Jews were only allocated 253 calories of food per person, compared to 2,613 for Germans. Jews were forbidden to step outside the ghetto and any Pole caught aiding a Jew was killed on the spot.

Within the ghetto Jews ran a *Judenrat*, or 'Jewish Council', and police, schools, libraries and theatres to keep up spirits, until the Nazis forced councillors to choose who should fill quotas for deportation to death-camps. The decision drove many an official to suicide.

WORLD WAR

Hitler's 1939 Polish invasion triggered World War II, which led to Germany invading Norway and Denmark in April 1940, and France, Belgium, Holland and Luxembourg in May. All but Britain fell before the German *blitzkrieg*, or 'lightning war'. Meanwhile, Italy and Japan joined Germany in a Tripartite Axis Pact in September. In July 1939 the Nazis had shut down the *Reichvertretung der Juden in Deutschland*, or 'National Agency for Jews in Germany', a compulsory organization of all Jews in the Reich headed by Rabbi Leo Baeck, and replaced it with a National Association directly run by the Gestapo. Jews in conquered countries were subjected to Nazi race laws, and wartime exigencies meant that emigration was no longer possible.

FRANCE AND ALGERIA

From July 1940 France was divided into a German-occupied zone in the north and the puppet Vichy regime in the south, which collaborated with the Nazis and deported thousands of Jews to German camps.

The Crémieux Decree of 1870 had naturalized Algerian Jews, but that status was revoked when 117,000 Jews felt the weight of the racist Vichy laws in Algeria.

THE RUSSIAN FRONT IN 1941

Having conquered most of mainland Europe, Adolf Hitler turned his attention eastwards. On 22 June 1941, he breached his non-aggression pact with the Soviet Union and launched Operation Barbarossa, which caught millions of Jews in a fatal dragnet. Nazis decapitated Jewish leadership by murdering any Communist commissars they found, and killing all but one or two of Lithuania's 300 communal rabbis.

RESISTANCE FIGHTERS

During April–May 1943, Mordechai Anilewicz (1919–1943) led the first armed Jewish resistance to Nazism in the Warsaw Ghetto uprising. Somehow the residents resisted for five weeks, before succumbing to Nazi soldiers, who razed the site at the cost of 7,000 Jewish lives. The remaining 50,000 were sent to concentration or extermination camps.

Later the Vilna Ghetto rose up and resistance groups formed in Bialystok, Minsk and Kovno ghettos. In Poland, Jews commanded 4 of the 12 partisan units parachuted in in 1944. Despite such bravery, nothing could stop the murder of millions known as the Holocaust.

Below *A searing image of infamy: Nazi troops round up Jews after crushing the 1943 Warsaw ghetto uprising.*

HOLOCAUST – FINAL SOLUTION

THE HOLOCAUST IS REGARDED AS THE ARCHETYPAL EXAMPLE OF MAN'S CAPACITY FOR WICKEDNESS. FROM A JEWISH PERSPECTIVE, NAZI RACIAL GENOCIDE PROVED MORE LETHAL THAN ANY ANTI-SEMITISM IN HISTORY.

The Holocaust, or *Shoah* in Hebrew, destroyed Jewish human life on a scale never seen before, eliminated Europe as a leading centre of Jewish civilization, and left an irreparable wound on the Jewish psyche.

Jews were not the only sector of European society to suffer the Holocaust. An estimated 500,000 Roma and Sinti gypsies were also killed, as were homosexuals, mentally and physically disabled people, the 'Rhineland bastards' (offspring of Germans and African soldiers from World War I), and political opponents, including dissident churchmen. Yet Jews were pursued with unparalleled fanaticism and died in far greater numbers.

THE 'FINAL SOLUTION'

SS chief Heinrich Himmler created *Einsatzgruppen*, or 'action forces' before the war to round up and kill Jews, gypsies and Communists. Now their commandos killed Jews on the spot as they ploughed through Ukraine and the Baltic states *en route* to Moscow. Officials sought a more comprehensive approach. On 31 June 1941 Hitler's deputy, Hermann Goering, entrusted the Reich Security overseer, Reinhard Heydrich, with implementing 'a complete solution to the Jewish question', affecting an estimated 11 million Jews throughout the German sphere. Jewish emigration was totally prohibited on 31 October 1941. In January Heydrich convened a conference at Wansee, near Berlin, to co-ordinate the logistics of total extermination. Heydrich was assassinated in May 1942 but the policy lived on.

A NETWORK OF CAMPS

In Germany the prototype concentration camp was Dachau, set up near Munich in 1933. All extermination camps, a 1942 innovation, were located outside the Reich. The six most infamous were in Poland: Auschwitz, Chelmno, Belzec, Majdanek, Sobibor and Treblinka. Others were located in Croatia (Jasenovac), Ukraine (Janowska) and Belarus (Maly Trostenets).

Prisoners sent to such camps were not expected to last more than 24 hours. Conditions were also atrocious in 'conventional' camps – 70,000 died in Bergen-Belsen and 56,000 in Buchenwald. In 1942 Germany began mass deportations from ghettos at a bewildering pace, as part of Operation Reinhard: 300,000 Jews were shipped over just 52 days from the Warsaw Ghetto to Treblinka, where in total 750,000 Jews were killed.

GAS CHAMBERS

As early as 1933 the Nazis had used carbon monoxide to achieve the 'euthanasia' of physically or mentally handicapped people. But this method was inefficient – hence gas chambers using faster-acting Zyklon B were invented.

Above *The view that greeted US soldiers after they liberated Buchenwald concentration camp, April 1945.*

Left *Jewish women and children marked with the yellow star are forced on to cattle truck trains to the death camps.*

The selection process, as to who would die immediately or be forced to work, took the form of a pseudo-medical inspection. Jews selected for death were sent to take 'showers' in rooms that were actually gas chambers, and died within 25 minutes. The Nazis tattooed prisoners with a number on their arm; no one was addressed by name; and badges distinguished groups – yellow star for Jews, pink triangle for homosexuals.

AUSCHWITZ

Based on an old Polish military barracks near the town of Ozwickiem, Auschwitz mutated in 1942 into the largest death camp of all. It became a fully fledged city with street lighting, railway tracks and electrical and plumbing systems. An additional site was added, called Birkenau, plus a factory at Mona. Thirty freight cars of Jews arrived every day.

After victims died, a unit called the Sonderkommando purloined gold teeth, shoes, bones, even human fat which was sent to soap factories, and hair, for stuffing pillows.

***Below** Prelude to the Holocaust: German soldiers face a synagogue set ablaze by locals after the Nazis occupied Lithuania, 1941.*

THE STATISTICS

The following are estimates of the numbers of Jews killed in the Nazi Holocaust and the percentages of each country's pre-war Jewish population who died.

Country	Killed	%
Poland	3,000,000	90%
Soviet Union	1,250,000	44%
Hungary	450,000	70%
Romania	300,000	50%
Germany/Austria	210,000	90%
Netherlands	105,000	75%
France	90,000	26%
Czechoslovakia	80,000	89%
Greece	54,000	77%
Belgium	40,000	60%
Yugoslavia	26,000	60%
Bulgaria	14,000	22%
Italy	8,000	20%

All suffered collective punishment if anyone escaped, and many froze to death standing in punishment grounds. Attached to Auschwitz was a unit that experimented on live human beings. Allied airplanes overflew Auschwitz, but were ordered to bomb more militarily valuable targets. Overall, some 1.5 million Jews perished at Auschwitz.

HUNGARY AND GREECE

In April 1944 the Holocaust reached Hungary, on the back of the Nazi invasion. Until then, Hungarian Jews bore burdens but their lives were safe. Immediately Adolf Eichmann, one of the major organizers of the Holocaust, began sending Jews to Auschwitz; 380,000 arrived over six weeks and 300,000 died. Even when the Soviet Army stood at the gates of Budapest, the Germans managed to arrest 40,000 Jews and sent them on a death-march to Auschwitz.

THE FEW WHO HELPED

Certain German-occupied nations distinguished themselves by resisting, such as Finland; Denmark, which smuggled most of her Jews to neutral Sweden; Italy, which flouted German deportation edicts; and above all Bulgaria, where resolute government action saved 50,000 Jews. It is also said that King Mohammed of Morocco personally refused to hand over Jews to the Vichy overlords.

***Above** Raoul Wallenberg, the Swedish diplomat who risked his life to save thousands of Jews in Hungary.*

A few brave individuals helped Jews at great personal cost. In late 1942 Jules Géraud Saliège, Archbishop of Toulouse, publicly protested against Vichy French deportations. 'All is not permissible against them. They belong to mankind. They are our brethren as are so many others. No Christian can forget that', he wrote.

Another saviour was Raoul Wallenberg, a Swedish diplomat in Hungary who saved perhaps 15,000 Jewish lives by issuing false papers.

French Protestants and Catholics in Le-Chambon-sur-Lignon hid Jewish children during 1942–44. And Oskar Schindler, a Sudeten German industrialist, rescued almost 1,200 from certain death by getting them transferred from Auschwitz to work in his factories. Sadly, such cases were the exceptions; most people just averted their gaze.

THE AFTERMATH OF GENOCIDE

WHETHER THE HOLOCAUST WAS THE ZENITH OF CENTURIES OF ANTI-SEMITISM, OR A WARTIME ABERRATION, WHEN STANDING BEFORE THE MURDER OF SIX MILLION JEWS, PERHAPS THE MOST FITTING RESPONSE IS SILENCE.

One by one, the death camps were liberated by Allied troops: Auschwitz by the Red Army on 27 January 1945, Buchenwald by the US Army on 11 April, and Bergen-Belsen by the British Army on 15 April.

NUREMBERG TRIALS

From November 1945 to October 1946, an International Military Tribunal put 24 pre-eminent Nazi leaders on trial within the US occupation zone. The location was Nuremberg, doubly fitting because it was the site of the Nazi mass rallies and the Nazis' first systematic racial legislation. Questions were raised about the complicity of ordinary Germans and whether personnel acted on orders from above or on their own initiative.

Below *'Never again' was the pledge made at the Nuremberg International Military Tribunal, where Nazi perpetrators of crimes against humanity were put in the dock, January 1946.*

PSYCHOLOGICAL TRAUMA

Jews, too, faced troubling questions: notwithstanding a few uprisings, why had so many been led 'like lambs to the slaughter'? Thousands felt guilty for surviving when relatives had perished, or strove to hide the degradation from their children. Memories of impossible moral choices, like having to decide which child to surrender to the Gestapo, deepened their trauma.

Mostly, Jews felt cheated by Western civilization and the allure of its supposed 'enlightenment'. Survivors who returned to their countries were often shocked by their reception. When in July 1945 200 Jews arrived in Kielce in Poland, local anti-Semites launched a pogrom that killed 42 of them. This massacre convinced Jews that they had no future in Europe. Many tried to escape to America, while thousands joined the *Beriha*, or underground 'flight', of 1944–8 to southern Europe, *en route* to Palestine. An estimated 50,000 reached Palestine during these years, despite a British bar on entrance.

Above *A memorial wall in Krakow, constructed of Jewish gravestones that had been destroyed by the Nazis.*

DISPLACED PERSONS CAMPS

Among the eight million people displaced by World War II were some 50,000–100,000 Jewish camp survivors. Another 150,000 Jews soon joined them after fleeing anti-Semitism in Romania, Poland, Russia and Hungary. From October 1945 the newly established United Nations set up a relief administration to run displaced persons (DP) camps in Germany. Meanwhile, the group *Sh'erit Ha-Pletah*, or 'surviving remnant', met in congress at Munich in February 1946 and elected representatives for Jews who had nowhere to live.

BEHIND THE IRON CURTAIN

The Kremlin ignored the anti-Jewish nature of Nazi actions. If anything, Russian anti-Semitism increased after the war. In August 1952, 13 leading Yiddish poets were executed. Jews were called 'rootless cosmopolitans' and 'American agents' in the official press. Soon hundreds of Russian Jews lost their jobs or were arrested, the zenith being the supposed 'Doctors'

Above *Jewish women and children at Belsen concentration camp, Saxony, where British troops found 60,000 barely alive survivors.*

Plot' against Stalin. During the Cold War, Soviet authorities banished Jewish activists to the Gulag, and effectively barred ordinary Jews from various professions and universities.

Europe's post-war division into an American-sponsored western bloc and a Russian-backed eastern bloc also had adverse ramifications for Jews. Jews in eastern Europe found themselves subject to the same strictures as those in the USSR. They could not leave since Communist governments barred emigration. Worse, Jews were purged from Communist parties throughout the region, culminating in the arrest and execution of Czech party secretary Rudolf Slansky and 11 other leading Jews in November 1952.

PERPETRATORS, VICTIMS AND BYSTANDERS

During genocide, argued the historian Raul Hilberg, everyone is a perpetrator, victim or bystander. To blame German culture uniquely ignores non-German bystanders. A survey of 1941 shows that even before the Holocaust got under way, various peoples were persecuting Jewish citizens. French police arrested 4,000 Parisian Jews and interned them in urban Drancy, near central Paris. Over three years, 65,000 were deported from there, of whom only 2,000 survived. Likewise, Lithuania's 'Order Police' began exterminating Jews as soon as the Soviets left; and in September 1941 Ukrainian collaborators helped Nazi *Einsatzgruppen*, or deployment groups, shoot 33,771 Jews and dump their corpses at Babi Yar, a ravine near Kiev, in the largest single massacre of the Holocaust.

MEMORIALS

As early as 1945, Zionists met in London to plan a project to commemorate the Shoah (Holocaust in Hebrew). The result was the complex known as Yad Vashem (hand of God), which was built over 200 acres in Jerusalem. An avenue recalls the 'Righteous' gentiles who risked their lives to save Jews from death.

People also recall the Holocaust's acts of quiet courage, such as when prisoners held secret religious services, even when many asked, 'Where was God in Auschwitz?'

Israel has long held an annual Holocaust Day; now the UN and other nations do the same. In America, several museums mark the genocide. Berlin's Jewish Museum, opened in 2001, features a poignantly empty Holocaust Tower. Berlin also inaugurated a sculptural Memorial to the Murdered Jews of Europe in 2005.

BIRTH OF ISRAEL

The United Nations was founded in 1945 to banish genocide and replace war with dialogue. No doubt these factors hastened the decision to set up the State of Israel in the former British Mandate of Palestine in 1948. To many Jews, the fact that only three years elapsed between the Holocaust's end and the birth of the first Jewish state in 1,900 years was a miracle. But even this triumph cannot lessen the worst disaster to befall Jews in their history.

Below *Displaced persons encampment, Bamberg, where thousands of survivors spent the immediate post-war years.*

CHAPTER 5

ZIONISM, JERUSALEM AND ISRAEL

Political Zionism was one of several ideologies that gained credence among Jews in the late 19th and early 20th centuries. Nor was it initially the most popular. In 1948, however, just three years after the Holocaust wiped out a third of all Jews, the United Nations acceded to Zionist pressure and promulgated Israel as the first Jewish state in 1,900 years. Since then, Israel has outgrown its austere beginnings, revived Hebrew as a living language, and fulfilled the Biblical prophecy of 'gathering in the exiles', including most Jews from Europe and the Middle East. Triumph came at a cost, however. Israel has endured numerous wars and is blamed for dispossessing Palestine's indigenous Arabs. In addition, its acquisition of territories after 1967 encouraged settlers whose messianic fervour has stoked controversy. None the less Israel is today culturally vibrant and economically powerful. Demographically it has probably overtaken the United States as the major centre of modern Jewry.

Opposite *Israeli flags flutter at a religious ceremony held at the Western Wall, Old City of Jerusalem. The men wear tallit and tefilin according to ancient Jewish custom.*

Above *David Ben-Gurion, the first Prime Minister of modern Israel. He became premier two days after Israeli independence in May 1948.*

ZIONISM – THE NATIONALIST DIVIDE

TURKISH MILITARY DEFEAT AND BRITAIN'S BALFOUR DECLARATION ENCOURAGED ZIONISTS TO REVIVE THEIR FADING MOVEMENT. DESPITE RESISTANCE, THEY PRESSED FOR A NATIONAL HOME IN PALESTINE.

Two events in 1917 rescued Zionist fortunes: the Balfour Declaration of 2 November, which expressed British governmental support for establishing a 'national home' for Jews in Palestine, and General Allenby's British military conquest of Jerusalem on 11 December. The prime mover behind the Balfour Declaration was Chaim Weizmann. As head of a Zionist delegation to the Versailles peace talks of 1919, he proclaimed that peaceful Jewish autonomy alongside Arabs in Palestine was both possible and necessary. In April 1920 the San Remo conference awarded Britain with mandates to govern Mesopotamia (Iraq) and Palestine, with the Balfour Declaration incorporated into the latter's charter.

Below *A Labour Zionist poster for May Day, 1945, proclaims in Hebrew: 'Workers of all peoples, unite!'*

Not all Jews were convinced that Zionism answered their most perplexing questions. Was Jewish nationalism really the best option? If so, was Palestine the place to locate it? And if Zionism was the way, which type should prevail out of the many contending strands?

ORTHODOX VERSUS SECULAR VIEWS

Until 1789 Jewish political and religious identity had essentially been one; after the French Revolution, Jews gained civil rights and members of the Haskalah (Jewish Enlightenment), began to redefine themselves in social and national as well as religious terms. Secular Zionism grew out of such views, yet drew heavily on imagery from the Torah, Talmud and daily prayer liturgy – nostalgia for the days of Jewish kings, rediscovering ancient Jewry's agrarian past and the mystical concept of redemption and negating the disharmony of exile.

Most Orthodox Jews prayed daily for a return to Zion, which they believed lay in the Creator's hands alone. They saw political Zionism as blasphemous because it was driven by humans, not by God's hand. They felt that the resultant community would be secular, not religious, so not a truly 'Jewish state'.

RELIGIOUS DISSENTERS

Denial of Zionism on religious grounds inspired the first truly global Orthodox political group, World Agudat Yisrael (Jewish Union), founded in Kattowicz, southern Poland, in 1912. A smaller contingent of religious Zionists had already since 1902 organized themselves as Mizrachi – an acronym standing for 'religious centre'. They argued that faith without national spirit was only 'half Judaism'. Mizrachi affiliated with other Zionists, relocated to Palestine in 1920 and set up a youth wing, Bnei Akiva, nine years later.

Above *Theodor Herzl with Zionist delegation on board* Imperator, *on the way to Palestine, October 1898.*

At the opposite end of the religious spectrum, Reform Jews opposed Zionism for different reasons. They saw Judaism as a system of ethical principles and nothing more; nationality ought to depend on where one lived, not ethnic ties. Nazi oppression made many German Reform Jews reappraise that position.

BRITAIN'S VIEW

There are many theories as to why Britain backed Zionism, such as its desire to guard Middle East routes to India, or to ward off German or French aspirations. The Anglo-Jewish establishment was itself split down the middle on the Zionist issue. The leading Liberal politician Edwin Samuel Montagu considered Zionism a 'mischievous political creed'. The deliberate ambiguity of the Balfour Treaty's phrase 'national home' – not 'state'

– is often attributed to Montagu's watering down of the more strongly phrased original promise.

REBELLION

Before Balfour, diplomatic disappointments had deepened rifts within the Zionist movement. Some accused Theodor Herzl (1860–1904), the founder of political Zionism, and his successors of defining Zionism too negatively, as a cure for the disease of anti-Semitism. Frustrated at lack of progress over Palestine, the British Zionist Israel Zangwill had split from the Zionist movement at the 7th Congress of 1905 to lead his breakaway Territorialist group, which sought alternative homelands in Africa, Asia and Australia, but the group withered away in 1925. There were also differences between activists in Palestine versus the bureaucrats in Berlin and London; and between political Zionists, who stressed settlement before all else.

SOCIALIST ZIONISTS

More successful was a socialist party called *Po'alei Zion*, or 'Workers of Zion', and the young Russian-born David Ben-Gurion became its chief activist. To his left were Zionists of a more fiercely Marxist hue, who saw their trend as part of a global class struggle. After 1909 some young socialists began setting up *kibbutzim*, or 'collective farming colonies', and championed what they called 'Hebrew labour'. They co-operated with Arthur Ruppin, who in 1908 had founded the Zionist Organization's Palestine Bureau.

ARAB RESISTANCE

A few Palestinian Arabs welcomed the economic boost brought by Jewish immigration, but when the influx grew their suspicions increased. Arabs disliked the alien nature of Zionist socialism and felt that the 'Hebrew labour' policy discriminated against them in the workplace. Palestinian Arab newspapers such as *Karmil* (founded in 1908) ran campaigns against selling land to Zionists, and *Filastin* (1912) decried increased Jewish immigration. Above all, Arabs feared that Europeans might usurp or outnumber them.

Between 1873 and 1914 the Ottomans replaced the old administrative unit, *Jund Filastin*, or 'Palestine Province', with three separate *vilayets*, or 'governorates'. Most Palestinian Arabs, however, referred to themselves as part of Greater Syria. In

Above *David Ben-Gurion signing the State of Israel document, 14 May 1948, marking the end of the British Mandate.*

January 1919 their delegates attended a General Syrian Congress in Damascus that rejected Zionism, as well as a French mandate over Syria. They wanted to see Palestine incorporated within a united independent Syria and join the Arab delegation at the Paris Peace Talks.

Also in January, Chaim Weizmann met Emir Faisal, Sharif of Mecca and putative Arab leader. The two signed agreement for mutual cooperation, but this proved void when Britain and France, in Faisal's view, reneged on promises to grant him a kingdom.

A US commission of inquiry led by Henry King and Charles Crane in 1919 interviewed Jews and Arabs and provided a report that opposed major Jewish immigration. It also advised against a Jewish national home in Palestine, which could lead to 'dispossession of non-Jewish inhabitants'. Their views notwithstanding, the perils of anti-Semitism in 1920s Europe and especially the rise of Nazism in the 1930s continued to drive thousands of Jews to Palestine.

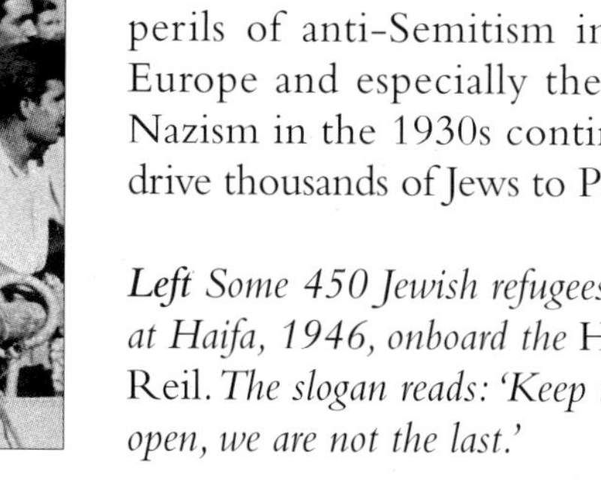

Left *Some 450 Jewish refugees arrive at Haifa, 1946, onboard the* Haviva Reil. *The slogan reads: 'Keep the gates open, we are not the last.'*

Palestine During World War II

Zionists were pulled in different directions during the war. Many fought with British units, others terrorized British targets in, or smuggled refugees into, Palestine.

In early 1939, with world war looming, Britain hosted a last ditch attempt to solve the Palestine problem. London hoped to reconcile the competing demands of the Jews who had been promised a homeland in the Balfour Declaration and the Palestinian Arabs who were resident in the region.

Concerned that Arab nations might side with Germany and Italy, on 17 March, London released the McDonald White Paper, which dropped the Peel partition plan of 1938 and vowed to establish an independent and unitary Palestine by 1948. The paper also restricted Jewish immigration to 75,000 over the five-year period, 1940–44. Palestine's Jews did not welcome a unitary state where Arabs would outnumber them by 1.2 million to 550,000. However, Jews feared Germany more than they resented Britain for breaking past promises.

***Below** Erwin Rommel, the 'Desert Fox' who dreamt of leading German forces through North Africa to Palestine.*

PALESTINE'S JEWS IN WORLD WAR II

In late 1940, 26,000 Jews and 6,000 Arabs joined a British infantry division in Palestine nicknamed the 'Buffs' (the East Kent Regiment). Britain also helped create the Palmach in May 1941, a strike force of the Zionist militia, Haganah, to counter Nazi threats to Syria and Lebanon. Even the militant Irgun, the Revisionist Zionist underground, ceased sniping at Mandate forces and supported Britain's war effort.

BEHIND ENEMY LINES

Palestinian volunteers showed remarkable courage in Europe, despite criticism that they should have acted sooner. In 1943 the Budapest-born Hannah Szenes, a poet and playwright, was one of 33 who parachuted behind enemy lines in Slovakia and the Balkans, teamed up with anti-Nazi resistance fighters and sought out beleaguered Jewish communities. In June 1944 she crossed into her native Hungary, but was captured, tried and executed in November. In September 1944 the British formed the 5,000-strong Jewish Brigade, which fought in Italy and helped Jews in German Displaced Persons (DP) Camps after the war. Their military skills were passed on to Haganah, or the Socialist Zionist underground militia.

***Above** Three young Jewish survivors of Buchenwald concentration camp, en route to Palestine.*

SMUGGLING IN 'ILLEGALS'

Haganah cadres now started smuggling in *ma'apalim* ('illegal Jewish refugees) from war-torn Europe. Over 100,000 tried to enter Palestine on 120 boats in an operation dubbed 'Aliyah B', and 70,000 succeeded. There were setbacks too: the British blockaded the coast and interned 50,000 would-be immigrants in Cyprus, Mauritius and Atlit prison, Palestine.

In November 1940 Haganah seized an illegal vessel, the *Patria*, with 1,800 refugees on board. When the British threatened to divert the refugees to Mauritius, Haganah saboteurs bungled an attempt to disable the ship and it sank off Haifa, killing 267. Survivors stayed in Palestine as 'an act of grace'.

OPTING FOR STATEHOOD

As the attempted annihilation of Europe's Jews entered its final stage, Zionist and non-Zionist Jewish groups agreed on a common strategy. At an emergency meeting in New York's Biltmore Hotel in May 1942, delegates declared the goal of a Jewish state, or 'commonwealth', in all of Palestine, which exceeded the terms of the Balfour Declaration.

Above *Jewish pilot training school near Rome in November 1948, when the newly formed Israel Air Force was still in combat against Arab foes.*

SEASON OF TERROR

In 1940 the Polish-born Revisionist Abraham Stern had formed Lehi, an underground unit also dubbed the Stern Gang. Lehi attacked British forces during the war, unlike fellow Revisionists in Irgun.

With war still raging in Europe, on 1 February 1944 Irgun declared its own 'revolt' against Britain. Its leader was Menachem Begin, who served in the Polish army in 1941. At first, Irgun sabotaged police stations and tax offices in Tel Aviv, Haifa and Jerusalem. Irgun and Lehi soon moved from sabotage to terror, and in August 1944 Lehi tried but failed to assassinate the British High Commissioner for Palestine, Harold McMichael. Two Lehi hitmen shot dead Lord Moyne, British Minister Resident in the Middle East, on 6 November 1944 in Cairo. This was a step too far for the Jewish Agency. They barred Lehi and Irgun members from jobs, and, in what was dubbed the Saison (season), Haganah and Palmach helped the British round up dissidents.

ANGLO-AMERICAN COMMISSION

The appalling images of Nazi death camps after World War II ended in May 1945 had radicalized Jewish feeling. Operation *Beriha* began siphoning 'illegals' from eastern Europe to Palestine via secret land routes. Lehi and Irgun blew up oil pipelines in Palestine, and after July the Haganah suspended the Saison and joined its former foes in a joint Resistance Movement that launched 19 attacks over ten months.

An Anglo-American committee of inquiry spent four months in 1945–6 interviewing Jews in Displaced Persons (DP) camps in Vienna and Arabs in Cairo. Their unanimous report of April 1946 proposed the immediate entry of 100,000 Jews into Palestine; an end to the land purchase restrictions of 1940; and the eventual establishment of a bi-national state under United Nations trusteeship. Britain's premier Clement Attlee said Jews could only enter Palestine when Zionist and Arab militias were disarmed. Even so, 1,500 Jews were let in each month after October 1946, half from detention camps on Cyprus, to the anxiety of Palestine's Arabs.

ANGER AT THE BRITISH

Fury over British policies prompted the worst act of Jewish terrorism, the Irgun's July 1946 bombing of Jerusalem's King David Hotel, site of the Palestine government secretariat and British military headquarters. In total, 91 people died. A curfew was imposed on the Jewish area of Haifa.

One of Britain's last acts during its mandate over Palestine helped push the UN towards making Israel independent. When in July 1947 the chartered ship *Exodus* entered Palestinian waters with 4,500 Holocaust survivors from European Displaced Person (DP) camps on board, British naval vessels trailed and eventually boarded the ship. Encountering aggressive resistance to their taking over the vessel, British soldiers resorted to force. Three passengers were killed and 30 wounded. Would-be illegal immigrants were eventually sent back to DP camps in Germany, and the *Exodus* became a media *cause célèbre*, symbolizing Jewish desperation to reach Palestine.

Below *King David Hotel bombing, 1946, when Jewish saboteurs destroyed the British Army HQ, killing 91.*

THE WAR OF INDEPENDENCE

THE UN'S DECISION TO GRANT SEPARATE STATES TO JEWS AND ARABS WAS WELCOMED BY MOST JEWS, BUT REJECTED BY ARABS WHO WANTED ONE STATE. WAR SAW ZIONISTS DEFEND THE FLEDGLING ISRAEL.

On 29 November 1947 a United Nations General Assembly (UNGA) voted by 33 to 13 to split Palestine into two states, one predominantly Jewish, the other Arab. The USA and Soviet Union voted for partition, while Britain abstained. Generally, Zionists accepted UNGA Resolution 181, while most Arabs, both in Palestine and the region, rejected it.

FIRST STAGE OF WAR

Within hours of the UN vote, fighting broke out between communities. By January, Arabs were blockading Jerusalem and an Arab Liberation Army entered Palestine. By March, 1,200 Jews had been killed. On 9 April Irgun and Lehi militants invaded Deir Yassin village near Jerusalem and killed at least 100 civilians. Four days later Arabs attacked a convoy of Jewish doctors and patients and killed 80. Arab flight from Haifa and Jaffa gathered pace, and in early May Safed and Jaffa fell to Zionist forces. Most of west Jerusalem was now in Jewish hands, while the Jewish settlement of Gush Etzion fell to Arabs.

Below *A convoy bringing supplies to Jews in Jerusalem, 1948, during the siege by Jordan's Arab Legion.*

INDEPENDENCE

On 12 April 1948 David Ben-Gurion formed a provisional cabinet. War was now inevitable, and future Israeli prime minister Golda Meir made a secret deal with King Abdullah of Jordan. Zionist forces would only minimally attack areas in the eastern half of Palestine (West Bank), an area officially reserved for a Palestinian state but coveted by Jordan in exchange for control over all of western Palestine.

On 14 May 1948 the Jewish state in Palestine, now called the State of Israel, declared its independence. The declaration proclaimed 'the natural right of the Jewish people to be masters of their own fate, like all other nations' and pledged 'equality of social and political rights to all inhabitants irrespective of religion, race or sex.' Ben-Gurion vetoed any mention of specific borders. In a rare moment of concord, the USA and Soviet Union both recognized Israel.

ARAB ARMIES INVADE

As soon as independence was declared, five countries attacked Israel – Syria, Lebanon, Jordan, Egypt and Iraq. The Israelis made gains, except in Jerusalem, which fell to Jordan, and in the Golan, which fell to Syria.

Above *Jewish youths marching in Jerusalem on 30 November 1948, the day after the United Nations' decision to establish a Jewish State.*

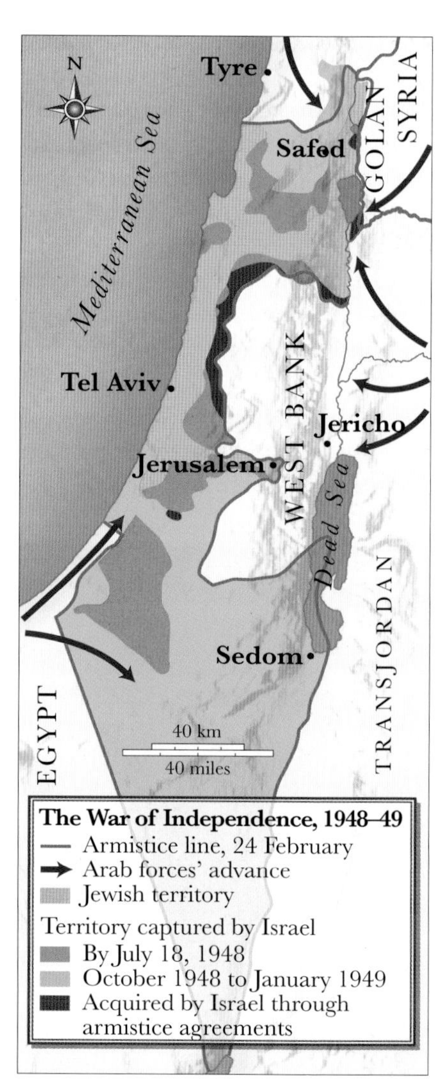

Right *During the war, Israeli forces rebuffed attacks from Egypt, Jordan and Syria, and gained new territory.*

On 31 May, Israel's government announced the official disbanding of all separate pre-state Zionist militias. Their members would be subsumed within a single organization, the Israel Defence Forces (IDF), which had 100,000 troops by the year's end. While the IDF held the Syrians at bay in the north, it could not break the siege of Jerusalem until 10 June, when a secret bypass, 'Burma Road', was opened through the Judean Hills.

TRUCES AND CONFLICTS

The UN effected a truce on 11 June and sent Count Folke Bernadotte, a Swedish diplomat who had rescued 21,000 Jews during World War II, to Palestine. Bernadotte proposed that Palestine be annexed to Jordan, with a Jewish enclave attached to assist Arabs economically. Palestinian Arabs and Jews rejected the idea.

Fighting resumed on 9 July with Egyptian attacks in the south, battles in the north, assaults on kibbutzim and Israeli conquests of Lydda, Ramle and Nazareth. A second truce began on 19 July and, on 16 September, Bernadotte released his second plan. This time he acknowledged Israel as a reality, though he recommended awarding the Negev to Egypt and Jordan. His report called for 360,000 Arab refugees to be allowed to return home. The next day Lehi gunmen shot Bernadotte in Jerusalem. Mufti Hajj Amin Husseini's Government of All Palestine was declared in Egyptian-run Gaza, as was a pro-Jordanian Palestinian Congress in Amman, Jordan. Neither was truly independent. In 1950 Jordan formally annexed the West Bank, a gesture only Britain and Pakistan recognized.

The second truce ended on 15 October, after which the IDF relieved Negev settlements, took Beersheva, wiped out the Arab Liberation Army, and, according to Israel's 'new historians', units killed civilians in several Arab villages. In December, Israel entered the Sinai Desert and in March 1949 it secured the southern Negev, including the crucial port of Eilat.

Armistice talks opened on 12 January 1949, and Israel signed agreements with Egypt, Lebanon, Transjordan and Syria. The new state added 50 per cent to the territory allocated to it under the UN plan and linked up split areas.

Many reasons may explain the course of the war including divergent interests and poor strategic co-ordination between Arab forces and secret aid from Diaspora Jewry. For the first time in almost 2,000 years there was a Jewish state, the fulfilment of long-held dreams and a place of refuge for victims of future persecution.

FIRST ELECTIONS AND THE LAW OF RETURN

Israel held its first Knesset (parliamentary) elections on 25 January 1949. In March, David Ben-Gurion became Israel's first prime minister. His coalition government included his Mapai labour party and smaller factions, including a Sephardi list, Arabs from Nazareth and a United Religious Front. Begin led the opposition and Chaim Weizmann became state president after Albert Einstein declined.

THE REFUGEE CRISIS

The 1948–9 War of Independence was seen as a victory for Jews. To Palestinians, however, it was known as the *nakba*, or 'disaster'. Their leaders had rejected the UN partition plan and lost the war, and some 725,000 Palestinians fled the country. Israel now controlled 77 per cent of historic Palestine and 60 per cent of Palestinian people became refugees.

Areas to which most Palestinian Arabs migrated included the West Bank; Gaza Strip; Lebanon; Syria; Transjordan; Egypt and Iraq.

Many of the 190,000 Arabs who stayed in Israel but left their homes are 'internally displaced'.

As of 2008, a million of Gaza's Palestinians live as refugees. The refugee question constitutes one of the 'final status issues' still at stake in Israeli–Palestinian peace talks.

In July 1950 Israel's Law of Return granted all Jews the right to immigrate as a defining principle of the nation.

Having survived possible annihilation, the young state faced the challenge of absorbing immigrants and maintaining security. Yet peace has remained elusive ever since.

***Right** Socialist Zionists defending Kibbutz Gal-On from Egyptian forces, in the southern Negev Desert, 1948.*

JEWISH DEMOGRAPHY AFTER WORLD WAR II

SINCE 1948 OVER 3 MILLION JEWS HAVE SETTLED IN ISRAEL. YET DIASPORA COMMUNITIES HAVE SURVIVED AND EVEN BLOSSOMED, ADDING TO THE EVER-CHANGING MIX OF JEWS THE WORLD OVER.

Jewish life altered dramatically in the 20th century. Before World War II some 8.5 out of 10 million European Jews lived in a generally backward eastern Europe and developing Soviet Union. A further 300,000 Jews lived in Asia, 500,000 in Africa and 400,000 in Latin America. Some two-thirds of Jews resided in chastened conditions. After the war, three-quarters of Diaspora Jews resided in advanced countries, USA, Canada, western Europe and a now developed USSR. Comparative affluence and acceptance led Jews to adopt national languages, spelling the demise of Jewish tongues such as Yiddish, Ladino and Judeo-Arabic.

In a history with extraordinary highs and lows, the Jewish people probably experienced more upheaval in the 20th century than ever before. The decimation of the Holocaust, birth of the State of Israel and unprecedented immigration utterly transformed Jewish demography.

There were about 4.75 million Jews globally in 1850, 8.7 million in 1900, 13.5 million in 1914 and 16.6 million in 1939. Today, Jews worldwide total 13 million, 0.23 per cent of the earth's population compared with 33 per cent who are Christians and 20 per cent who are Muslims.

Below *In 2012 US President Barack Obama hosted his fourth Passover Seder in the White House, Washington DC.*

QUESTIONS OF DEFINITION

The debate over who constitutes a Jew partially explains the statistical ambiguities. Normative Jewish religious law, *halakha*, defines a Jew as someone born of a Jewish mother or someone who converts to the faith.

Reform Judaism in the USA opposed intermarriage in 1909, and again in 1947. In 1950 just 6 per cent of American Jews married non-Jews, but by 2000 that figure had risen to 40–50 per cent. In 1983 Reform acknowledged social changes and accepted patrilineal descent. This made it difficult for Orthodox or Conservative Jews to marry Reform Jews. In the same way, 'patrilineal Jews' wishing to settle in Israel may be accepted for citizenship by state law, but they are still deemed non-Jewish when it comes to marrying other Jews.

Above *Author Maxim Gorky by Isaac Brodsky, a Russian member of the Jewish Society for the Encouragement of the Arts.*

IMMIGRATION TO ISRAEL

Within Israel, the Jewish populace has grown at least eightfold from 650,000 in 1948. Some 1.5 million Israeli citizens are Palestinian Arabs; and in the territories occupied after 1967 there live at least 3.5 million Palestinians, Muslim and Christian, including a large proportion of refugees from pre-1948 Palestine.

SOVIET JEWS IN GERMANY

Germany attracted droves of Soviet Jewish immigrants after the unification of East and West Germany in 1990. Germany's Jewish population currently stands at about 200,000, the third largest in Europe after

France and Britain, and the fastest growing on the Continent. Former Soviet citizens now make up most of Germany's Jews, and feel under-represented on the Zentralrat, the Central Council of Jews in Germany. Founded in 1950, it is a bastion of indigenous German-speaking Jews, many of whom are descendants of Holocaust survivors. It favours Orthodox Judaism while Soviet Jews, estranged from their roots after 70 years of Communism, prefer US-style Reform founded in 1997.

MIDDLE EAST

During the 20th century, Jews in the Middle East region underwent a demographic revolution: their numbers rocketed from half a million in 1900 to more than five million in 2000, but the distribution of that population was massively skewed. In 1900 most Middle Eastern and North African Jews lived in Iraq, Yemen and Morocco, with smaller pockets in Egypt, Syria, Algeria, Tunisia and Libya. Sizeable minorities also existed in non-Arab countries, Turkey and Iran. After 1948, virtually all Arab states saw their Jewish populations rapidly diminish and in some cases disappear altogether.

Israel was the chief beneficiary, and by 2000 about 95 per cent of the region's Jews dwelt in that one country. Turkey, Iran and Morocco retain Jewish communities of more than 10,000, but these are exceptions to the rule and even there they are a fraction of their size a century ago.

ISRAEL AS THE JEWISH HOMELAND

Above Israelis celebrate Independence Day with a picnic in the park, 2010.

Owing to immigration, Israel's population nearly doubled in its first five years. Jews leaving displaced person camps in Germany were followed by thousands from the Middle East. Absorption camps became permanent towns with persistent social problems, leading to charges of an Ashkenzi discrimination against Jews from Arab lands.

One of the hallmarks of Israel is the way the state and rabbinate reached a 'status quo' from earliest days. Rabbis accepted national laws on most matters, but retained influence over law concerning marriages, burials and questions of identity. Most Israeli Jews are secular, but civil marriage is not allowed so non-believers still require rabbinical blessing for weddings.

Once the 1970s economic crisis was resolved, Israel adopted a more free enterprise system in imitation of America. Agriculture declined compared to industry and high technology. Unfortunately, the competitive economic atmosphere has resulted in increased disparities between rich and poor.

Most Diaspora communities cherish Israel and regard attacks on the country almost as attacks on them. Yet only a tiny minority of US, British or French Jews have emigrated to Israel. Some liberal Jews are critical of Israeli policies and some wish to distance themselves from Israel altogether.

EUROPE TRANSFORMED

At the end of World War II most surviving Jews on mainland Europe were found among the 250,000 located in displaced persons camps. A large number left for Israel, Britain, South America, Canada or the United States. Because Hitler never managed to invade England, Britain became by default home to the largest Jewish community in Europe, although its size has gradually declined since the 1960s. Since then the French community has grown into Europe's largest as Maghrebi (North African) Jews flocked to Paris, Marseilles and other cities.

But Jewish populations in the Czech Republic, Slovakia, Austria, Poland and Hungary are shadows of their former selves. After the 'Iron Curtain' came down in eastern Europe, migration was banned, Zionist groups were outlawed, and only a few intrepid souls managed to get out.

NEW SELF-CONFIDENCE

In short, the Holocaust and Cold War divisions transformed the face of Jewish Europe. Other than France, the only country that saw a marked increase in Jewish population after 1970 was, of all places, Germany.

Jews worldwide worry about renewed anti-Semitism which sometimes goes with anti-Zionism. Yet very few face the threats or legally sanctioned prejudice of the past. Most Jews feel financially secure and professionally fulfilled. That this should be so after the Holocaust is particularly impressive.

CHAPTER 6

JEWISH CULTURE IN MODERN SOCIETY

Most of today's 13 million Jews live in Israel and the USA. While genocide, turmoil and emigration have depleted eastern European and Russian Jewry, other European countries, such as France and Britain, have varied, creative Jewish populations; and Germany, once the birthplace of Nazism, is Europe's fastest-growing community of all. After centuries of discord, Jewish–Christian relations improved dramatically with the passage of the 1964 papal declaration, Vatican II. Jews today contribute to humanity through medicine, science and psychology; and express themselves via myriad paths, from the kibbutz and women-only prayer services to social activism, Jewish cuisine, an Orthodox revival and a plethora of hybrid identities. Individual Jews have depicted modern life in stimulating, sometimes disturbing, ways in art, philosophy and literature. Others pioneered cinema, television, orchestral music and rock bands, or invigorated traditional klezmer and Ladino musical forms. Similarly, synagogue design provides exciting contemporary casings for an ancient faith and ever-adaptable culture.

Opposite *After the travails of World War II, both tragedy and hope seem to inform this striking portrait,* Jewish Girl*, painted by the Italian artist Armando Pizzinato in 1945.*

Above *Moroccan Jews at a celebration honouring the medieval philosopher Maimonides. Today the UK-based Maimonides Foundation fosters relationships between Jews, Christians and Muslims.*

ISRAEL IN THE MODERN WORLD

BUFFETED BY WARS AND CRITICIZED FOR ITS ACTIONS, THE STATE OF ISRAEL HAS SURVIVED FOR 60 YEARS, ABSORBING IMMIGRANTS AND REDEFINING JEWISH HISTORY.

More than 60 years after its foundation, the State of Israel is militarily strong, economically robust and culturally vibrant. Israel probably now houses more Jews than any other nation on earth. In the words of a Second Aliyah song, Jews came to the land 'to build and be rebuilt', and in many respects that is what has been fulfilled.

HERZL'S DREAM REALIZED?

Jews from every continent have settled in the 'ancient homeland'. Reports say that Israeli Jews, 76 per cent of the population, grew by 300,000 in 2006–7, while the Jewish Diaspora shrank by 100,000. The very existence of the state has altered Jewish history. For the first time in 2,000 years, Jews can stand in the courts of nations and speak for their own national interests.

Jews outside Israel take pride in her considerable achievements in art, science, medicine and literature, on the battlefield, in trade and agriculture, and in her aid to Third World nations. They see everyday life of a Hebrew-speaking nation as a realization of Theodor Herzl's (1860–1904) dream of normalization. Religious Jews welcome the chance to live with dignity and to practise their faith on ancestral soil.

PERSISTENT TROUBLES

However, in many respects Israel remains a dream unfulfilled. Some 60 per cent of Jews still live in the Diaspora. Social disparities have grown, and inter-Jewish ethnic and religious tension remains an issue. Israel's Arab minority – descendants of those indigenous Palestinians who did not leave in 1948 – feel increasingly estranged, while Israel's conduct in the territories she occupied in 1967 has drawn wide criticism.

Most of all, Jews hoped that Israel would be a safe refuge; yet in view of the five major wars that have taken place since independence, two Palestinian *intifadas*, or uprisings, and recurrent terror attacks on its citizens, Israel has sometimes seemed like the least safe place for Jews.

Above *For a nation built on immigration, the Ethiopian Jewish exodus of the 1980–90s reminded many Israelis of their raison d'être.*

The Israel/Palestine question remains one of the most vexed political issues in the world. What began as a local dispute has been cast as a clash between East and West, and it has acquired religious overtones. Some Arab analysts call it the root cause of all Middle East troubles, while growing numbers challenge Israel's very right to exist.

FROM 1948 TO 1956

Israel endured years of economic austerity and hardship as it absorbed Jewish immigrants in its first decade – 500,000 between 1948 and 1950 alone. The 1950 Law of Return opened the doors to Jews everywhere. Conversely, in that same year Israel's Absentee Property law foreclosed Arab refugees' hopes of returning, which neighbouring Arab

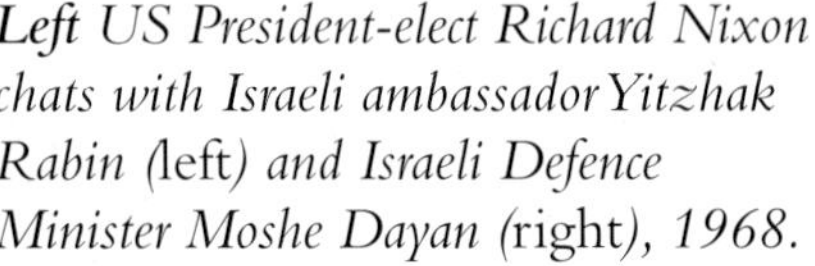

Left *US President-elect Richard Nixon chats with Israeli ambassador Yitzhak Rabin (left) and Israeli Defence Minister Moshe Dayan (right), 1968.*

leaders made a precondition for further talks. As a result, hopes receded of turning the armistice agreements that Israel signed in 1949 with Jordan, Egypt, Syria and Lebanon into full peace treaties.

Increasingly, Third World and Soviet bloc nations have portrayed Israel as an alien colonial outpost. Palestinian refugees on Israel's borders stepped up attacks as *fedayeen*, or 'self-sacrificers'. Israel's retaliations were often condemned as disproportionate. Egypt's post-1954 leader, Gamal Abdel Nasser, made 'Palestine' central to his pan-Arabist doctrine.

ROAD TO THE SIX-DAY WAR

All these factors raised tensions and set the scene for the October 1956 Suez War, in which the Israel Defence Forces (IDF) captured the entire Sinai and the Gaza Strip. However, UN and American pressure forced Israel to surrender all gains within a year.

In the 1960s Israel drew closer to Washington, and was alarmed when Egypt sponsored the creation of a Palestine Liberation Organization (PLO) in 1964. When Egypt blockaded the Gulf of Aqaba to Israeli shipping, Prime Minister Levi Eshkol (1895–1969) ordered a pre-emptive attack on Egypt, Syria and Jordan on 5 June 1967. In six days Israel defeated all Arab forces and quadrupled the size of land under its control. Up to 200,000 Palestinians became refugees.

A NEW PARADIGM AFTER 1967

In Israeli and Jewish eyes, David had defeated Goliath. Israel now held the Gaza Strip and the Golan Heights (Syrian). Most significantly it controlled the formerly Jordanian-run West Bank, what religious Jews call Judea and Samaria, the heart of biblical Eretz Israel. This included East Jerusalem's Old City with its Jewish Quarter, Temple Mount and Western Wall. However, Israel was now cast as an occupier, which in turn bred serious internal schisms.

Liberal Israelis envisaged trading territories for peace with Arabs – essentially the idea behind UN Security Council Resolution 242, which Israel signed in 1970. Others felt that expanding Israel's pre-1967 pencil-thin 'waist' would protect against future attack. Few Israelis, though, proposed annexation, as this would enfranchise Palestinian residents and erode the Jewish nature of the state.

Positions soon polarized: in August 1967 the Arab League rejected talks while the PLO recommitted itself to armed struggle. Within Israel buoyant religious Zionists felt that God had delivered victory, and considered it sinful to return an inch of sacred soil.

Above *The Suez Canal blockaded by sunken ships, a symptom of war, November 1956.*

YOM KIPPUR WAR

Many Israeli policy-makers believed they were invincible after 1967, although a draining 'war of attrition' with Egypt, between 1967 and 1970, should have warned Jerusalem against complacency. In October 1973 Egypt and Syria launched a pincer attack on Israel on Yom Kippur, the Jewish Day of Atonement, and caught the IDF unawares. Israel withstood the blows and after three weeks repelled the enemy, but more than 2,600 Israelis died in combat and national morale was badly dented.

The war prompted the resignation of Golda Meir, the first female premier in the region. It also gave new impetus to Jewish civilians who planted new settlements in the territories, often defying the prime minister, Yitzhak Rabin (1922–95), and contravening international law. A new movement, *Gush Emunim*, or 'Bloc of the Faithful', used messianic religious motifs to champion the settlers. Opposition crystallized in the Peace Now movement, which wanted to return Israel to its former 1967 'green line'.

Jews in Germany and Eastern Europe

Russia, Poland and Germany were once the heartlands of Jewry. Mass emigration and calamities in the 20th century seemed irreversible, yet shoots of revival have reappeared.

After taking control of Russia in 1917, the Bolsheviks dismantled the despised Pale of Settlement and outlawed anti-Semitism. Jews gained access to education and new professions. Leon Trotsky, Lev Kamenev and Grigori Zinoviev reached the highest echelons of Soviet power.

Liberation came at a price: the authorities banned Torah classes, confiscated religious property and had shut down half the synagogues by 1934. Jews who backed Zionist, Bundist, liberal or social-revolutionary parties faced persecution; even the Communist Party's Jewish division, the Yevsektsiya, was liquidated in 1930.

SHTETL CULTURE

The flight to the cities loosened bonds to the *shtetl*, the semi-rural heartland of Russian Jewry. New political borders divided formerly interconnected communities on the borderlands of Russia, Ukraine and Poland. The *shtetl* structure survived civil war pogroms and Stalinist totalitarianism. Yet what Communism did not extinguish, World War II did.

The Nazi–Soviet Pact of 1939–41 imposed a news blackout. When the Germans invaded in late 1941 it was too late for Jews living between Poland and Russia. Nazi *Einsatzkommandos* and local cohorts began the Holocaust with the mass shooting and gassing of 1.5 million Jews in western Soviet Union.

AFTER WORLD WAR II

Barred from fleeing south or west, many Jews went east, which saved lives but destroyed social cohesion. The Jewish Anti-Fascist Committee encouraged a brief cultural revival after 1943, but five years later Stalin had its leaders killed as traitors. The Kremlin barred publication of the 'Black Book', first-hand reports of Nazi atrocities against Jews, lest it detract from the preferred version of the 'Great Patriotic War'.

Above *Jewish Socialist Workers Party supporters celebrate revolutionary times under a Yiddish banner; Russia, 1918.*

NEW DISCRIMINATION

Israel's military victory in 1967 intensified anti-Zionism in Russia and officially approved attacks on Judaism itself. University quotas for Jews reduced their presence from 18 per cent of Soviet scientific workers in 1947 to 7 per cent in 1970. Under Brezhnev not one Jew was admitted to Moscow University in 1977–8. Some 250,000 were allowed to emigrate in 1971–4, after which the doors closed and 'refuseniks' (those refused an exit visa) were jailed on bogus security charges.

COLLAPSE OF THE UNION

The collapse of Communism across Europe in 1989 and the break-up of the Soviet Union in 1991 created a ripple effect on Jewish life in the region. Mass migration to the USA and Israel ensued, and some predicted the demise of Jewish life in Russia itself. Today most former Soviet Jews live in Israel, followed by the USA, with the Confederation of Independent States

Left *Austria finally returned Gustav Klimt's portrait of her aunt to Maria Altmann in 2006. In all, Nazis stole six of her family's artworks in 1938.*

Above Soviet Jewish refugee families reach Vienna on their journey out of the USSR, 1979.

(successor to the USSR) taking third place. It is thought about 300,000 Jews now live in Russia, 122,000 in Ukraine and 25,000 in Belarus.

Predominantly Muslim former Soviet Central Asian states have not discriminated against Jews. However, most Jews have emigrated, leaving behind small, aging populations. Only 3,600 Jews remain in Lithuania, once the centre of Jewish religious life.

EASTERN EUROPE

Throughout eastern Europe the events of World War II reduced once-vibrant Jewish communities to fractions of their former size. Thousands left for Israel and the West. The most dramatic decline was in Poland, whose pre-war population of 3.3 million Jews, accounting for 27.2 per cent of all city dwellers in 1931, had shrunk to 5,000 by the 1980s. Many Jews who had survived the Holocaust fled Hungary after the violent suppression of an anti-Stalinist revolt in late 1956.

Czechoslovakia's Jews played a leading part in the Communist establishment in the early days, and Czech arms helped a nascent Israel survive the 1948 war. Then in 1952 party secretary Rudolf Slansky was accused of being a crypto-Zionist, ousted, and executed along with 11 other Jews. Three years later Czechoslovakia became the chief conduit for Warsaw Pact weapons to Israel's Arab neighbours. This switch in policy fed Israel's sense of entrapment, and in part persuaded her to side with Britain and France in the Suez War of 1956.

Two organizations represent the Jews of a newly united Europe: the European Council of Jewish Communities, first established in 1968, and the European Jewish Congress, founded in 1986. Since 1996, 26 European countries have participated in an annual European Day of Jewish Culture. In an event scarcely imaginable just ten years earlier, Poland, Hungary, Slovakia, the Czech Republic, Slovenia, Latvia, Lithuania and Estonia all joined the European Union in May 2004, and Bulgaria and Romania followed in January 2007. As a result Jewish communities in the West and East began meeting each other again after decades of division.

GERMAN RESETTLEMENT

The country that truly defied expectations was Germany. Jews have settled there in large numbers. Most come from the former Soviet Union and many others are Israeli; by 2000 they outnumbered the German descendants of Holocaust survivors, who in 1950 had set up a *Zentralrat*, Central Council, to rebuild their community. West Germany taught schoolchildren about the Holocaust, and after 1952 paid reparations to Jewish survivors for wartime suffering and property stolen, totalling $25 billion by 1987. Bonn also established firm relations with Israel and offered former refugees German citizenship.

Right Once a symbol of a divided Europe, the Berlin Wall's ruins now stand for future hope of tolerance and lasting peace. Photographed in 1989.

VATICAN II

Relations between Roman Catholics and Jews took a turn for the better in 1965 with the rulings of a council called Vatican II. The key document, *Nostrae Aetate*, 'In Our Time', proclaimed: 'Jews should not be presented as rejected or accursed by God.' The Church, 'mindful of the patrimony she shares with the Jews', condemned persecution of Jews and for the first time absolved them for killing Jesus.

East Germany was less forthcoming about acknowledging wartime crimes, so Jews were wary at the prospect of reunification after the Berlin Wall came down in 1989. But Jewish life is mostly thriving.

THE AUSTRIAN CONUNDRUM

Austria saw itself as 'Hitler's first victim' and unlike Germany denied guilt for killing its Jews. There was scandal over the alleged SS wartime record of Austria's 1986–92 president, Kurt Waldheim. Vienna's Jewish population fell from 200,000 pre-war to 8,000 by the 1980s, but Jews have since made a positive impact on post-war Austrian life.

THE SPREAD OF JEWISH COMMUNITIES

GLOBALIZATION IS NOTHING NEW FOR JEWS WHO LEFT EUROPE AND THE MIDDLE EAST TO MAKE NEW LIVES IN SOUTH AMERICA, SOUTH AFRICA, AUSTRALIA, HONG KONG AND SINGAPORE.

Today four out of every five Jews live in either Israel or the United States. Of the remaining 2.3 million, 550,000 are found south of the US–Mexican border. Paradoxically most of these Spanish- and Portuguese-speaking Jews are not Sephardi but Ashkenazi.

Tighter US influx controls made South America more attractive after 1924, and drew immigrants from far and wide. This created great variety: Venezuela with its 35,000-strong half-Ashkenazi, half-Sephardi community; Uruguay with 40,000 Jews in 1980; Cuba, reduced from 12,000 pre-revolution to 1,000 today, and Guatemala, home to many German Jews. In Mexico, 45,000 European, Damascene and Sephardi Jews have largely moved from commerce to the professions. 'Judaizing' sects of *mestizos* (half-Indians) claim Jewish ties.

Below *Daniel Barenboim, born in Argentina in 1942, conducting the Arab-Jewish Divan Orchestra, 2010.*

Right *Templo Libertad, Buenos Aires, a synagogue that symbolizes Judaism thriving south of the equator.*

South American states helped pass the 1947 UN Partition Plan that created Israel, spawning strong intercontinental ties ever since.

JEWS OF ARGENTINA

Argentina accounts for nearly half the continent's Jews. Its Italian and Spanish inhabitants attracted 88,000 Jews in 1901–14, and another 74,000 Russian Jews in 1921–30 joined groups from Morocco and Syria.

Anti-Semitism rose with German encouragement in the 1930s, though 30,000–40,000 refugees from Nazism entered Argentina during 1933–43, many illegally. Post-war Argentina absorbed former Nazis and in 1966 the military junta sacked civil servants who were Jewish. In 1967 nearly half the world's anti-Semitic incidents occurred in Argentina and 1,500 Jews are still counted as 'missing', presumed killed by the state. In 1994, 85 people were killed in a terrorist bombing on the Asociación Mutual Israelita Argentina in Buenos Aires , the centre of the Argentinian Jewish community.

Today, Jews are well integrated and contribute to society, arts and sciences, especially since the end of junta rule.

BRAZILIAN JEWS

Unreliable figures suggest millions of Brazilians have 16th-century Jewish or Marrano (crypto-Jewish) ancestry. Moroccan Sephardim founded a synagogue in Belem in 1824; but today's community of about 150,000 are mainly of Russian, Polish and Hungarian descent. Communal activities started in Porto Alegre in 1910 and soon extended to São Paulo and Rio de Janeiro, where most Jews now live. Jews also farmed on ICA communes along the Rio Grande, though by 1958 most had left for the cities. Each wave of immigrants brought its own flavour. Some 24,000 Jews arrived from west and central Europe in 1931–39 and 12,000 from Arab countries in 1957–60 joined an existing 5,000-strong Egyptian-Jewish community in São Paulo.

SOUTH AFRICA

Although South African Jews number fewer than 71,000, just 0.5 per cent of the population, their impact remains significant. The community is known for its strong Lithuanian origins. The youth groups Habonim, Beitar and Bnei Akiva nurtured Zionist ties, and per capita South African funding of Israel exceeds all other Diaspora communities. Until the recent building of yeshivas (academies), and renewed religiosity in Johannesburg, all chief rabbis were imported from Britain.

Rabbis and community heads were slow to condemn apartheid, but individual Jews helped lead the anti-apartheid struggle, including Ronnie Kasrils, Albie Sachs and Joe Slovo. For 13 years, Helen Suzman was a lone parliamentary voice against official racism.

Some 40,000 Jews had left before black majority rule was attained in 1994. Many pursued careers in Britain, including the former attorney for Nelson Mandela, now Law Lord Joel Joffe; and much earlier the future Israeli foreign minister Abba Eban, and Lord Solly Zuckerman, chief UK science advisor.

Below *Consecrated in 1863, the Old Synagogue, Cape Town, is the oldest in South Africa.*

Since 1994 fear of crime and reduced employment opportunities have seen Jews move to Australia. Some 80 per cent of emigrants leave with university degrees, whereas few of their Lithuanian forebears had finished secondary school. By the same token former Zimbabweans and Israelis are replenishing South Africa's otherwise aging community.

AUSTRALIA AND NEW ZEALAND

Today, South African and recent Soviet immigrants make up nearly a quarter of Australian Jews. They joined British Sephardim, who developed businesses, galleries and libraries in the 19th century. Refugees from Germany revived a community that seemed to be losing its identity. Its population grew from 70,000 in 1968 to 120,000 in 2008. Australia has 81 synagogues, numerous day schools, low intermarriage rates and an above-replacement level of Jewish children.

Far smaller in size is the Jewish community of New Zealand, which numbered just 5,000 in the 1990s. Even so, 'Kiwi Jews' included Sir Julius Vogel, twice premier in the 19th century; and the novelist, Benjamin Farjeon, who edited the islands' first newspaper. Since then there have been many prominent Jewish doctors, hoteliers, retailers, university professors and steel industrialists.

Above *Twice Prime Minister of New Zealand, Sir Julius Vogel (1835–99) campaigned for women's suffrage.*

ASIA

Americans and Israelis boosted Hong Kong's Jewish population from 200 in 1974 to 4,000 in the 1990s. The first settlers were English- and Arabic-speaking Baghdadi Jewish traders, who also built a tiny, vibrant community in Singapore. One of their descendants, David Marshall, became the first premier of Singapore after independence in 1955.

In India, Baghdadi Jews represent a third wave of arrivals. Other Jews settled in Cochin in the 10th century. The Bene Israel of Bombay, known as 'Sabbath-observing oil pressers', claim descent from 3rd-century shipwreck survivors. India took in refugees from Nazi Germany and Poland, though after independence numbers fell from 45,000 to under 6,000, with many leaving for Israel. General Jack Jacob spearheaded India's victory in the Indo-Pakistan War of 1971. In 2012 he declared, 'I am proud to be a Jew, but am Indian through and through.'

WOMEN IN JEWISH SOCIETY

'PATRIARCHAL' JUDAISM IS OFTEN SEEN AS CHAUVINISTIC, YET EVEN ORTHODOX JEWS NOW STRIVE FOR GENDER EQUALITY. JEWISH WOMEN HAVE CONTRIBUTED GREATLY TO THE ARTS, SCIENCES AND PROFESSIONS.

While outsiders see discrimination against women in the ultra-Orthodox community, the Bible often suggests a different attitude. Women probably sang in Temple services and prayed with men at the Sanctuary in David's time. The matriarchs Sarah, Rebecca, Leah and Rachel are venerated as 'mothers of the Jewish people'. Moses' sister Miriam was called Israel's first prophet; the judge Deborah led in battle; and Queen Esther saved Jews from destruction in Persia. For all that, the abiding impression of the Old Testament is of a man's world.

Similar contradictions apply to Jewish practice. On the Sabbath a husband sings to his wife that she is a woman of worth; and the Talmud calls on a man to love his wife as himself and respect her even more. Yet there is a daily prayer for men to thank God for not making them women, and women in Orthodox synagogues cannot be rabbis, cantors or choristers. Separated from men by a *mechitza*, or 'barrier', they may not handle the Torah nor publicly recite from it, and cannot qualify for a *minyan*, or the quorum of ten men needed for a full service. Religious women hide their hair beneath *sheitls*, or 'wigs' or 'scarves'. Perhaps most controversial today is that Jewish law restricts women's activities during menstruation.

CHECKS AND BALANCES

Defenders of Orthodoxy argue that post-Talmudic checks and balances have guarded against sexist abuse. Formally a man may divorce a woman and not vice versa; yet the medieval Rabbeinu Gershom allowed women to petition a rabbinical council for an annulment and outlawed polygamy.

Women are exempt from many Torah commands because, argue the rabbis, they are innately more spiritual than men. They ruled that running the household equalled religious ritual. Many feminists see such attitudes as anachronistic and patronizing.

Above Biblical heroine Queen Esther with her uncle Mordechai. Dura-Europos mosaic, 2nd-century Syria.

HISTORICAL COMPARISONS

In the past, Jewish women were not necessarily more oppressed than Christian and Muslim women. Jewish women were powerful independent merchants in England after 1066 and Judaism insisted that all women be literate. Apart from converts, someone is only Jewish if their mother is; the father's faith is irrelevant.

RELIGIOUS REFORM

Enlightenment values wrought significant change in certain synagogues. Reform thinkers referred back to the gender equality presumed in Genesis: 'God created man in His own image; male and female created He them'. As a result, both men and women lead services, read from the Torah and sing in choirs at American Reform and some Conservative synagogues. In 1922, Reconstructionist Rabbi Mordecai Kaplan had his daughter Judith take the first bat mitzvah, equal to the bar mitzvah for boys. However, only in 1935 was Regina Jonas ordained as the first female Reform rabbi, in Germany.

Unlike strictly observant Haredi and Hassidic Jews, modern Orthodox have gradually tried to make women feel more a part of religious services. They adopted a variant of the bat mitzvah, and since the mid-1970s

WOMEN PIONEERS

Increasingly, Jewish women are being recognized for their contributions. Some changed history, such as Dona Gracia who led Portuguese refugees to Turkey and Palestine, and Tannait Asenath Barzani of Mosul, yeshiva head in 17th-century Kurdistan. Women like Rahel Levin in Berlin, Genevieve Straus in Paris and Ada Leverson in London hosted salons, a practice revived by Gertrude Stein and Alice Toklas in 20th-century America. Western feminism is unimaginable without Betty Friedan, Andrea Dworkin, Erica Jong and Naomi Wolf.

Prolific Jewish women writers have included the South African Nobel laureate and enemy of apartheid Nadine Gordimer; Emma Lazarus, Lillian Hellman and Cynthia Ozick in America; Margo Glanz of Mexico and Marjorie Agosin of Chile; and Shulamit Hareven and Shifra Horn in Israel. Prominent women scientists include Rosalind Franklin, who helped unveil the DNA double helix; and Italy's Rita Levi-Montalcini, 1986 Nobel laureate for discovering the protein that makes nerves grow.

Above Hannah Arendt, political theorist and the first female professor at Princeton University, in 1960.

Above Pioneering child psychoanalyst Anna Freud in 1927 with her father, Sigmund Freud, and her niece Eve.

a Tefillah Network has arranged separate women's prayer groups and 'partnership *minyans*' where they read directly from the Torah.

FEMINISM

Jewish women were extremely prominent in the post-1960s feminist movement, but few addressed specifically Jewish concerns. A more pointedly Jewish critique started with Trude Weiss-Rosmarin, an American educationalist whose seminal 1970 article, 'The Unfreedom of Jewish Women', inspired a group to change Jewish laws. Tamar Ross, Rachel Adler, Paula Hyman and the Reform thinker Judith Plaskow (author of *Standing Again at Sinai*) have since amplified her views.

Below A girl reads from the Torah for her bat mitzvah, initiation into the community equivalent to the bar mitzvah for boys.

PROMINENT THINKERS

Jewish women often helped define 20th-century trends in society at large. They range from the cult novelist Ayn Rand to the political theorist Hannah Arendt. Susan Sontag wrote radical essays on photography and popular culture, while Yale professor Seyla Benhabib of Turkey addresses issues of globalization and multiculturalism.

AMBIGUITIES IN ISRAEL

In Israel, women serve a mandatory two years in the army. The kibbutz demanded absolute gender equality. In 1969 Golda Meir became Israel's prime minister, the first woman premier in the Middle East. Israel adopted laws of affirmative action for women in 1993. Yet women's rights, championed by politicians such as Yael Dayan and Ada Maimon, usually play second fiddle to issues of war and security.

Today campaigners fight Orthodox strictures on women's right to pray at the Western Wall; others challenge new Hebrew words that betray sexist bias; and the New Israel Fund has shelters for battered women. Women in Black have long marched in solidarity with Palestinians, and Machsom Watch monitors abuses at checkpoints in the territories. In response, rightist settlers set up their own Women in Green.

Female Israeli and Palestinian legislators jointly demanded greater women's involvement in peace brokering in 2005. Sceptics may doubt their chances, yet the record of the Four Mothers lobby, which forced Israel to withdraw from Lebanon in 2000, suggests further surprises in future.

Below Israeli woman soldier, Jerusalem, 1990. Women have been part of Israel's military since 1948.

MEDICINE AND SCIENCE

THE JEWISH DOCTOR HAS LONG BEEN A RECOGNIZED FIGURE ALL OVER THE WORLD. THE OPENING OF UNIVERSITIES TO JEWS DURING THE 19TH CENTURY LED HUGE NUMBERS INTO THE SCIENCES.

In the Bible, God is called the great healer. Because mankind is seen as completing God's worldly plans, the doctor is regarded as performing divine work; Jews are obliged to value *peku'ah nefesh*, or 'preservation of life'.

Whole sections of the Talmud prescribe remedies and cures, and concern embryology, pathology and intricate examination of medical conditions. Jewish philosophers often practised medicine, such as the 9th-century master of ophthalmology and court physician to the Fatimid Isaac Israeli. Many rabbis combined their duties with medical practice. Maimonides, the most obvious example, wrote ten medical works including *Aphorisms of Moshe* and *Regimen Sanitatis*, written in Judeo-Arabic. His view that a healthy body is essential for a healthy soul influenced doctors for generations.

***Below** Jonas Salk (1914–95), whose invention of a safe and effective polio vaccine in 1952 has nearly eradicated the disease worldwide.*

FROM THE MIDDLE AGES TO THE 18TH CENTURY

During periods of liberality Jews studied medicine in the School of Salerno in 9th–12th century southern Italy, and at Jewish centres in 12th–13th century southern France. Jews served as physicians to Christian kings in Zaragoza, Toledo and Barcelona, and to Muslim sultans in Cairo and Cordoba. The 1492 Iberian expulsions disseminated Jewish medical knowledge to Holland, Germany, Denmark and the Ottoman empire.

MEDICINE IN EUROPE

Jews were still mostly excluded from the best European medical schools until two events dramatically changed matters: the Austrian Edict of Toleration of 1782 and the French Revolution of 1789. Jews poured into the universities and soon achieved remarkable successes. Tsarist edict still barred them from reaching their potential in Russia, and in Germany they were denied access to prestigious fields like surgery. None the less, they were pioneers in ignored areas – notably microscopy, neurology, biochemistry, haematology and psychiatry.

20TH-CENTURY BREAKTHROUGHS

Progress accelerated in the 20th century, although now the stress was on practical application of accumulated knowledge. Paul Ehrlich helped create chemotherapy and invented the first effective drug against syphilis in 1910; shortly after, Casimir Funk showed how vitamin B could counter beri-beri. Partially realizing Ehrlich's dream of a 'magic bullet' to destroy bacteria, the English Nobel Prize-winner Sir Boris Chain isolated penicillin, while other Jews, Harry Eagle and Maxwell Finland, pursued the new field of antibiotics.

***Above** Hans Krebs, German-born British doctor and biochemist who won a Nobel Prize in 1953.*

In America, Jonas Salk discovered the polio vaccine and in 1963 founded the famous Salk Institute for Biological Studies at La Jolla, California. Albert Sabin, a pioneer in immunology and the relationship of viruses to cancer, invented the oral polio vaccine, which largely eliminated the disease after it was publicly released in 1961.

PHYSICS

As with medicine, Jewish scientists, physicists and chemists flourished with the academic advances of the 19th century. Similarly, the advent of Nazism in the 1930s saw a decided shift in talent from old Europe to America. One early pioneer was the Breslau-born Arthur Korn, who transmitted the first photograph by wire. In the USA innovation and enterprise often went hand in hand, a prime example being Isaac Singer's famous sewing-machine invention, whose export to Britain in the 1860s boosted the still-nascent and Jewish-dominated tailoring trade.

There were few fields where Jews did not leave their mark. Abraham Sztern (1762–1842) pioneered early calculating devices, Siegfried Marcus (1831–98) invented an ignition device in 1864 and the first petrol-driven vehicle in 1870; David Schwartz (1852–97) built the first dirigible airship in 1896 (Count von Zeppelin bought the plans from his widow in 1898). Theodore von Kármán (1881–1963) pioneered supersonic aerodynamics, while Mikhael Gurevich, together with A.I. Mikoyan, built the first supersonic Soviet jet airfighters, the MiGs.

ALBERT EINSTEIN

Apart from creating the greatest upheaval in scientific thinking since Isaac Newton, Albert Einstein (1879–1955) became a prominent figure in Jewish affairs.

Einstein used his platform to criticize politicians and lambasted the abuse of science: 'In the hands of our generation these hard-won achievements are like a razor wielded by a child of three.' Einstein resigned his post at the Royal Prussian Academy of Sciences when Hitler took power in 1933 and never returned to Germany. Instead he travelled to Oxford, England, and eventually settled in Princeton, USA. He protested against the use of nuclear arms, although he was largely responsible for the technology that created the bomb.

Above *Two giants of nuclear physics conferring: Albert Einstein and Robert Oppenheimer.*

A Zionist who agitated for peace between Jews and Arabs, Einstein was offered the presidency of Israel in 1948 but declined. Always proud of his Jewish roots, he was an agnostic, although he said that 'The mysterious stands at the cradle of true art and true science'.

CHEMISTRY

Jewish scientists have found chemistry a particularly fruitful field. In 1916 Fritz Haber won a Nobel Prize for synthesizing ammonia. The Austrian Karl Landsteine discovered the basic blood groups and the Rhesus blood factor. In Israel, Aharon Katzir (Katchalski) gained world fame for his work in polymer chemistry, while his brother, Ephraim, an expert in proteins at the Weizmann Institute, created synthetic fibres for use in internal stitching, and became Israel's fourth state president (1973–8). Aaron Klug, a South African, won a Nobel for his study of the three-dimensional structure of nucleic acids, proteins and viruses.

Left *Italian neurologist and 1986 Nobel Medicine prize-winner Rita Levi-Montalcini celebrating her 100th birthday in style.*

THE LIFE SCIENCES

Jews in zoology, botany and biology included Julius Sachs, the creator of experimental botany; Lawrence Bogorad, professor of biology at Harvard; and Moses Ezekiel, one of the world's leading economic botanists. Waldemar Mordecai Haffkine developed the first effective vaccine against cholera in 1892. Otto Loewi and Sir Bernard Katz won Nobel Prizes for discovering how nerves work. From 1950 to 1967 Jewish scientists won 11 of the 46 Nobels for biology.

SPLITTING THE ATOM …

Jewish scientists, who won 48 of the 174 Nobel Prizes in the field during 1901–2004, have played a disproportionate role in atom-splitting studies, the best known of all being Albert Einstein. Another was Max Born, an early master of quantum physics and probability theory.

It was Einstein's letter to President Roosevelt that launched America's top-secret Los Alamos Manhattan Project and created the world's first atomic bomb. The Manhattan team included many great Jewish nuclear physicists, like the American Robert Oppenheimer, and Edward Teller, later credited with inventing the hydrogen bomb.

JEWISH ARTISTS AND THEMES IN ART

ART HAS LONG POSED A QUANDARY FOR JEWS: THE TALMUD PRAISES BEAUTIFUL HOLY OBJECTS BUT THE TORAH ITSELF FORBIDS THE 'GRAVEN IMAGE', THUS PRODUCING ART WAS SOMETIMES SEEN AS REJECTING JUDAISM ITSELF.

Although synagogues banned human images, Pharaoh, Moses, Egyptians and Israelites peopled the pages of illustrated Passover *haggadahs*. Calligraphy became a fine art, as did micrography, which formed patterns and pictures from tiny marginal notes in the Torah.

DAWN OF THE NAMED ARTIST

Notions of the named individual artist bypassed Jews, until Moritz Oppenheim (1800–82) began painting elegant portraits of Jewish notables and biblical themes in German Romantic tones. Polish-born Maurycy Gottlieb (1856–79) painted *Shylock and Jessica* and *Jews Praying on Yom Kippur.*

In Holland the contemplative Jozef Israels (1824–1911) was hailed as a reincarnation of Rembrandt. Max Liebermann (1847–1935) shocked German salons with his overtly Jewish painting of *Twelve-year-old Jesus in the Temple*, though he later became the doyen of genteel portraiture and landscapes.

REBELLION AND SUPPRESSION

In eastern Europe the 1881 pogroms bred not only works of despair, but also Lazar Krestin's defiant *Birth of Jewish Resistance* (1905). Not all Jews felt obliged to paint 'Jewish themes'. The work of pioneering Impressionists Camille Pissarro and Isaac Israels reflected little explicit Jewish content.

Paris fostered new trends during 1900–40 such as Fauvism, Cubism, Dadaism and Surrealism, attracting Russian Jews like Marc Chagall and Chaim Soutine and Sephardi Jews like Amadeo Modigliani (Italian) and Jules Pascin (Bulgarian). This 'Jewish School' varied in style from Modigliani's African inspirations to Soutine's anxious Expressionism; only Chagall depicted Jewish imagery. 'Were I not a Jew', he wrote in his 1931 autobiography, 'I would not be an artist at all.'

Stalinism and Nazism stamped out individual expression. In 1933 Nazis sacked Max Liebermann as president of the prestigious Berlin Art Academy. Work by Jews was judged 'degenerate' and all non-representative art was considered the handicraft of Jews, even if the artist was 'Aryan'. Paradoxically, this drove creative talents into exile where they spread their radical ideas.

***Above** Prolific and ever innovative, the artist Marc Chagall celebrates his 90th birthday in 1977.*

BRITAIN AND THE USA

A remarkable flowering of Jewish artists occurred in Britain at the turn of the 20th century. The movement's godfather was Sir William Rothenstein, an Impressionist painter and principal of London's Royal College of Art (1920–35). His most talented pupil was Mark Gertler (1891–1939), who never forgot his Jewish roots, as seen in *The Rabbi and his Grandchild* (1913).

In 1914 David Bomberg's London Group organized the first exhibition of modern Jewish artists. Two German Jewish painters arrived in Britain in the 1930s: Sigmund Freud's grandson Lucian, a leading Representational portraitist, and the earthy Expressionist Frank Auerbach. England's Cecil Roth was the first true historian of Jewish art.

American art took the lead in daring abstraction, such as the 'colour field' innovations of Mark Rothko and

***Left** Jacob Epstein's powerful group sculpture* Social Consciousness, *1954, stands today in Philadelphia.*

ART THAT SERVES FAITH

Jews have used art from earliest times, often in the service of religion. The *mezuzah*, a doorpost prayer case, can be made of wood, ivory, metal or even sculpted coloured plastic. Ashkenazic coverings for Torah scrolls are made from embroidered cloth, and silver breastplates, and Sephardi tik boxes from wood or metal. The Torah is decorated with silver crowns and bells and a *yad*, an ivory pointer shaped like a tiny hand. Jewish craftsmen decorate the Sabbath loaf cloth, twin candlesticks and spice boxes.

Over time calligraphers and miniaturists illustrated flowers and pretty scenes on the *ketubah* or 'traditional marriage document'. Particularly beautiful *ketubot* (pl.) were made in Bohemia, Italy, Egypt, Persia, Jerusalem, Yemen, India and Afghanistan. Other objects treated artistically include kiddush cups, Hannukah lamps, Passover plates and even circumcision tools.

Above The Rabbi and his Grandchild*, a compelling portrait by Anglo-Jewish artist Mark Gertler, 1913.*

Adolph Gottlieb. Pop artist George Segal (1934–) invokes classical Jewish topics, such as Abraham sacrificing Isaac.

THE SCULPTED IMAGE

Even more than painting, sculpture represented a special taboo due to its association with idols. The first Jewish pioneer was Vilna-born Mark Antokolski (1843–1902), whose early Realist sculptures depicted such scenes as 'The Talmudic Debate' and 'Jewish Tailor'. More modern in ethos, the American-born British sculptor Jacob Epstein (1880–1959) continually quoted biblical themes: Adam, the Sacrifice of Isaac, Genesis, and Jacob and the Angel. Even more influential was the Cubist sculptor Lithuanian-born Jacques Lipchitz (1891–1973), who escaped Paris for America as Nazis invaded in 1941.

LOOTED ART

During World War II the Nazis took 100,000 art pieces from France alone; some 60,000 were recovered, of which 45,000 were returned to their owners or heirs, invariably Jews. Reparation for lost or 'looted' art is a controversial issue now and has proven a good opportunity to re-inspect some fabulous gems. Ironically Germans seemed passionate for abstract art, or art by Jews, given what Nazi propaganda called it.

ART IN ISRAEL

Zionist ideologues wished to create a 'new Hebrew' on Palestinian soil. Biblical scenes inspired Jakob Steinhardt; Yemenite settlers and local Arab farmers caught Reuven Rubin's imagination. Both studied at the Betzalel art and crafts academy, named after Moses' master craftsman and founded in Jerusalem in 1906 by Boris Schatz, a court sculptor in Bulgaria. In 1965 Betzalel's gallery turned into the Israel Museum, now the world's largest repository of Israeli art. Since then, Israelis have moved from 'Jewish imagery' to more universal, individual and abstract concerns.

PHOTOGRAPHY

When US galleries admitted photographs by Alfred Stieglitz, other Jews, such as the French Surrealist Man Ray and Hungarians André Kertész and Laszlo Moholy-Nagy began turning craft into fine art. Several exploited photography's documentary potential, for example German-born Alfred Eisenstaedt and Budapest-born Robert Capa in *LIFE* magazine, or Roman Vishniac, who shot the last days of Europe's *shtetls* and Jewish quarters.

Mary Ellen Mark, Diane Arbus and Lee Friedlander intimately observed contemporary US life, and Judah Passow and David Rubinger have chronicled Israel at war and peace. Examples of creative commercial portraiture and fashion include the baroque style of Irving Penn, the psychological work of Arnold Newman, the experimentalism of Cindy Sherman (USA) and Jeanloup Sieff (France), and Annie Leibovitz's elegant, often ironic studies of celebrities.

Right *A chronicler of a lost world, photographer Roman Vishniac shot this image of a child in Warsaw, 1938.*

THE JEWISH IMAGE IN LITERATURE

By the late 18th century, Christian writers showed renewed interest in Jewish themes. Gottfried Lessing's German plays *The Jews* and *Nathan the Wise* championed dignified Jews in the face of prevailing bigotry; and romanticism about an ancient, persecuted yet talented people partly countered the anti-Semitic depictions of Jews of 19th-century England.

***Above** Fagin, Charles Dickens' villain from* Oliver Twist, *suggested a negative view of Jews as criminals.*

By contrast, stereotypes of Jewish swindlers persisted, perhaps the most famous being Shakespeare's Shylock in *The Merchant of Venice*. In the 19th century Charles Dickens introduced Fagin in *Oliver Twist*. Shocked when readers saw his depiction as anti-Semitic, Dickens introduced a more sympathetic character in his last completed book, *Our Mutual Friend*, called Mr Riah, 'the gentle Jew in whose race gratitude is deep'.

Literature often treated Jews sympathetically when they were few on the ground, but when their numbers increased the mood changed. In *The American Scene* (1907), Henry James complained of 'a Jewry that had burst all bounds...There is no swarming like that of Israel'. T.S. Eliot and F. Scott Fitzgerald indulged in commonplace anti-Semitism, though by the 1930s backtracked somewhat when such views were associated with Fascism.

One writer who championed the oppressed Jews of Russia was Maxim Gorky (1868–1936). Though not himself Jewish he defended Jewish rights during the 1903 Tsarist pogroms, and after the 1917 October Revolution, which he supported, he wrote his 1918 story *Pogrom*.

***Below** Isaac Bashevis Singer, first Yiddish novelist to receive a Nobel Prize for Literature, in 1978.*

AMERICAN WRITERS

Isaac Bashevis Singer was an exception who still wrote in Yiddish. In 1978 Singer became the first Yiddish author to win the Nobel Prize for Literature. Although located in a Jewish setting, Singer's writing discussed issues that affect all society.

Bernard Malamud's Jewish self-awareness shines through in *Dubin's Lives* and *The Jewbird*. 'Everybody is a Jew but they don't know it', he wrote, suggesting Western urbanites now share what used to be a Jewish preserve – displacement and the need to juggle multiple identities.

Canadian-born Saul Bellow, a 1976 Nobel laureate, became perhaps America's top literary stylist who dissected post-war alienation in *Herzog* and *Humboldt's Gift*. Chaim Potok's more populist books threw a spotlight on an Orthodox world long ignored by the US literati, while Joseph Heller, whose *Catch 22* was a cult best-seller, later wrote ribald works like *God Knows* about King David. Even Allen Ginsberg, Beatnik poet and Buddhist convert, drew on his Jewish roots in *Howl* and *Kaddish*.

Norman Mailer's works straddled journalism and fiction, starting with *The Naked and the Dead*, 1948, and essays on Vietnam protest, radicalism and conservatism. Probably most searing in his critique of contemporary Jewry was Philip Roth, with *Goodbye Columbus* and *Portnoy's Complaint*, full of sexual fantasies and jibes at a domineering mother.

ENGLISH AUTHORS

Israel Zangwill (1864–1926), known as the Jewish Dickens, wrote *King of the Schnorrers*, a comedy that shot a few broadsides at the Sephardi elite. His magnum opus *Children of the Ghetto* introduced the vibrant Jewish East End to a wider readership. Later Anglo-Jewish writers have included such bold voices as Howard Jacobson, who won the

***Below** South African writer, political activist and winner of the 1991 Nobel Prize for Literature, Nadine Gordimer.*

Above Arthur Miller, who received the Pullitzer Prize for Drama in 1949 for Death of a Salesman, *at the United States Jewish Culture Awards in 1995.*

Man Booker Prize in 2010 with *The Finkler Question*, Clive Sinclair and Linda Grant.

Commonwealth writers include the South African Dan Jacobson, who often depicts the Jewish immigrant experience, and Nobel laureate Nadine Gordimer, an early foe of apartheid (racial segregation), who won the Nobel Prize for Literature in 1991. Smaller numbers of South African Jews wrote in Yiddish, Hebrew and Afrikaans, while in India, Bnei Israel member Nissim Ezekiel was called the leading English-language poet.

RUSSIAN STARS

While in 1897 only 1.3 per cent of the Pale's Jews spoke Russian, the rest Yiddish, 100 years later that ratio was reversed. The trend accelerated after the Revolution and led to passionate writing in Russian from the likes of Isaac Babel, reporter of Jewish Odessa and the vanishing shtetl, and later Boris Pasternak, Vassily Grossman and Nadezhda Mandelstam. Born in Russia and expelled in 1972, Joseph Brodsky, Nobel laureate of 1987, settled in the USA where he stated: 'I am Jewish – a Russian poet and an English essayist'.

THE ITALIAN LEGACY

Italy's small Jewish population has produced an amazing number of authors. Giorgio Bassani in *Garden of the Finzi-Continis* showed wealthier Jews surprised by fascist race laws. Others wrote 'non-Jewish' gems, such as Carlo Levi's paean to peasant life, *Christ Stopped at Eboli*. Primo Levi strove to understand the other Jewish worlds he encountered as a prisoner in Auschwitz. Some call his understated works the most powerful Holocaust literature written. Italian Jewish authors also include Alberto Moravia, Elsa Morante, Cesare Pavese, Natalia Ginzburg and Italo Svevo.

ASHKENAZIM WRITING IN SPANISH

Latin American Jewish writers tend to display spiritual restlessness and a passion for justice. Jacobo Timerman, a Ukrainian-born Argentine and author of *Prisoner Without a Name, Cell Without a Number,* was jailed for his dissident writings. Alicia Partnoy wrote about her experiences as a political prisoner in Argentina in *The Little School*. Cultural anthopologist Ruth Behar writes about her experience as a Cuban Jewish woman.

PLAYWRIGHTS

Loved on both sides of the English-speaking Atlantic, Arthur Miller wrote plays with few overtly Jewish characters, although recognizable Jewish types. Another prolific dramatist who addressed social ills was Lillian Hellman. Her successors have since pricked the nation's conscience on issues from racism and Vietnam to AIDS and infidelity. More recently Yasmina Reza, the French-based daughter of a Persian father and Hungarian mother, both Jewish, won fame in English translation for *Art*, a pastiche of 1990s materialism.

***Right** British playwright and political activist Harold Pinter was awarded the Nobel Prize for Literature in 2005.*

***Above** Howard Jacobson, celebrated Anglo-Jewish writer and columnist, who won the 2010 Man Booker Prize for Fiction, for* The Finkler Question.

In Britain, leading playwrights of Jewish origin include Jonathan Miller, Mike Leigh and the Czech-born Tom Stoppard, renowned for witty philosophical dramas. Frantisek Langer was one of Czechoslovakia's leading interwar playwrights. Many musical writers of modern America were Jewish, such as Irving Berlin, Richard Rodgers, Oscar Hammerstein II and Stephen Sondheim, and Jews are well represented as directors and scriptwriters for radio and television drama series. Additionally, Jews have contributed disproportionately to cinema, perhaps the quintessential art form of the 20th century.

Hollywood and Beyond

Cinema developed from humble origins in the 1890s to become perhaps the defining art form of the 20th century, and from the start Jews were intimately involved in the industry.

At first promoters and producers, then directors, scriptwriters, actors and composers, by 1912 Jews had set up over a hundred production companies in California, and were pivotal to the creation of the eight super-firms.

RAGS TO RICHES

Almost to a man – and they were all men – the Jewish movie moguls were born into poverty. Carl Laemmle, the 10th of 13 immigrant children, managed a clothes shop before running a string of nickelodeons and in 1912 founding Universal, the first big studio. Louis Mayer joined the junk trade at 8, owned a New York theatre-chain at 22 and produced the epic *Birth of a Nation* in 1915, aged 30. Adolph Zukor, who founded Paramount Pictures in 1917, was born in Hungary, emigrated at 15 and peddled fur garments.

A similar rags-to-riches story applied to the Warner Brothers, sons of a Jewish cobbler from Poland. In 1927 they amazed the filmic world by harnessing new technology to produce the first 'talkie'. Starring Al Jolson, *The Jazz Singer* presented Jewish family dilemmas about tradition and assimilation to a mainstream audience. In the 1930s cinema blossomed. MGM's Irving Thalberg released *Mutiny on the Bounty* in 1936; and David Selznik produced the immortal box-office sensation *Gone with the Wind* in 1939.

FILMS ABOUT JEWISHNESS

Jewish themes became ever more rare, as moguls deliberately played down ethnic traits. The same cannot be said of Yiddish cinema, or of shorter American films that targeted Jewish immigrants. Three basic types prevailed: the ghetto melodrama, the historical pogrom saga and the vaudeville comedy. The Marx Brothers films of the 1930s used humour that was Jewish in origin, and made it universally popular, appealing to anyone who ever had to deal with petty bureaucrats.

Above *A Night at the Opera – brothers Groucho, Chico and Harpo Marx hamming it up in 1935.*

GERMAN CINEMA

By the 1920s, cinema had spread worldwide, and in Germany, Jewish producer Erich Pommer made *The Cabinet of Dr Caligari*, which set a benchmark for creativity. Fritz Lang directed *Metropolis*, a futuristic critique of industrial society, and *M*, a Kafkaesque murder drama starring a young Peter Lorre. Unlike their Polish cousins, German Jews fostered a cosmopolitan rather than a particularly Jewish sensibility.

Nazism decimated this short-lived flowering, and most Jewish directors, actors, producers and technicians left Germany for London, Paris, Amsterdam or Hollywood. Ernst Lubitsch had already come to America in 1923, and top directors and actors Josef von Sternberg, Billy Wilder, Erich von Stroheim, Fred Zinnemann and the Vienna-born Otto Preminger soon followed. Meanwhile German cinema produced anti-Semitic dramas such as *The Eternal Jew.*

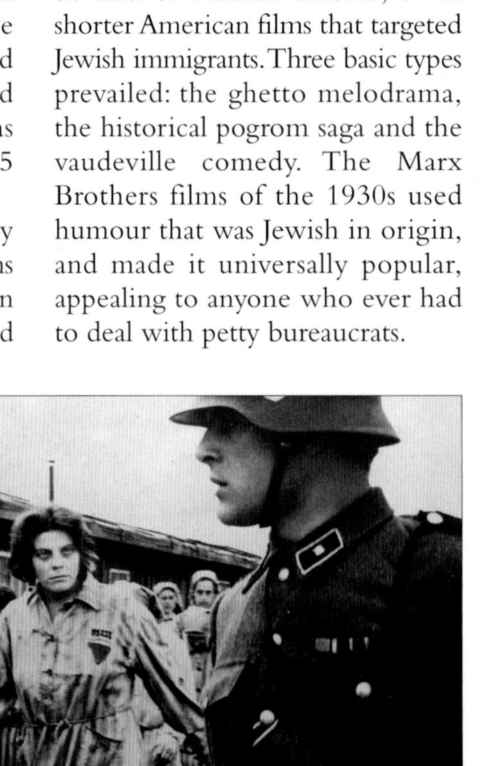

Left *Gillo Pontecorvo realized the power of cinema with his searing 1959 debut about the Holocaust,* Kapo.

Above Woody Allen faces Diane Keaton in his 1977 MGM comedic classic Annie Hall.

JEWISH HUMOUR

From the Yiddish writer Sholem Aleichem on paper to the earliest comic films, Jewish humour has been prized as characteristic of its people, even if at times it sails close to the edge of anti-Semitic typecast. What, though, makes it distinctly Jewish? One element is the *nebbish* or hopeless case. Since ghetto days the genre has been reincarnated in Marx Brothers and Woody Allen films.

Mel Brooks and Zero Mostel translated Jewish wit into zany and surreal films, Jerry Seinfeld pushed the boundaries of the television sitcom and the politically incorrect Jackie Mason still delights and shocks audiences. Meanwhile, Sandra Bernhardt, Sarah Silverman, Barbra Streisand and Goldie Hawn have mocked the image of the spoilt JAP (Jewish American Princess) or deliberately subverted the stereotype of the domineering 'Jewish mother'.

ÉMIGRÉS IN BRITAIN

British cinema received a boost from talented central European Jews such as Alexander Korda. He moved to Britain in 1930 and nurtured actors and films tailored to the American market, such as *Rembrandt, The Scarlet Pimpernel* and *The Third Man.*

Sir Michael Balcon graduated from Alfred Hitchcock films to Ealing comedies. Canadian-born Harry Saltzman produced the edgy *Look Back in Anger* (1959) and then a string of James Bonds. Karel Reisz, one of 669 Czech Jewish children who Sir Nicholas Winton rescued from the Nazis, defined the social realistic cinema of post-war Britain in *We are the Lambeth Boys, This Sporting Life* and *Saturday Night and Sunday Morning.* London-born John Schlesinger picked up the baton with *Billy Liar* and *Midnight Cowboy.* Other Anglo-Jewish directors are Michael Winner and Mike Leigh.

ISRAELI CINEMA

Most Israeli films have focused on a real Israel full of social tensions and ordinary concerns. The real maturation of Israeli cinema came after the 1967 war.

Directors have tackled such former taboos as the treatment of Holocaust orphans (*Summer of Aviyah*), Arabs and Jews in prison (*Beyond the Walls*), homosexuality (*The Bubble*) and the cost of war (*Avanti Popolo, Ricochets, Cup Final* and *Beaufort*).

JEWISH THEMES

After World War II many French, Italian, Czech and Polish film directors addressed Jewish themes. In his 1959 directorial debut, *Kapo*, Gillo Pontecorvo broached the awkward subject of Jews who collaborated or adopted false identities to survive the death camps. In France, *Le vieil homme et l'enfant* by Claude Berri focused on Jews who hid in wartime. After his light-hearted *Mazel Tov*, about a Jewish wedding, he won fame in 1986 with *Jean de Florette* and *Manon des Sources. Soleil* (1993), by Algerian-born Jewish actor-director David Hanin, began a trend of films about the North African Jewish experience.

The Diary of Anne Frank (1959) was the first Hollywood film to focus on the plight of Jews in the Holocaust; followed by *Judgment at Nuremburg* (1961). There was renewed interest in a pre-American past: *Fiddler on the Roof* revived nostalgia for the *shtetl* while recognizing its imperfections.

Jewish women appeared in the 1970s in a non-stereotypical way in *The Way We Were* starring Barbara Streisand, *Hester Street* and *Girlfriends.* New Jewish characters emerged: gamblers, lesbians, cowboys, hit-men and even whorehouse madams.

The comedies of Woody Allen and Mel Brooks turned the comic Jewish *nebbish* (hopeless case) into a representative of late 20th-century angst. *The Frisco Kid* (1979) showed Jewish values and American pragmatism clashing in the US. Steven Spielberg and Roman Polanski viewed the Holocaust anew with *Schindler's List* and *The Pianist.*

Below Film director Steven Spielberg with the cast of Schindler's List, *1993.*

MUSIC AND MUSICIANS

THE PROPHET ISAIAH PROCLAIMED, 'MAKE SWEET MELODY, SING MANY SONGS, THAT THOU MAYEST BE REMEMBERED'. FORBIDDEN FROM EXPRESSING THEMSELVES THROUGH THE GRAVEN IMAGE, JEWS TOOK TO MUSIC WITH ZEAL.

The songs of Miriam and Deborah are just two examples of early Jewish music. It has thrived, in both sacred and secular formats, while individual Jews have contributed immeasurably to Western classical, jazz, pop and folk.

The Bible and Talmud speak of elaborate musical arrangements associated with Temple rites and sacrifices, and even singing 'duty rosters' for Levite choristers. Performances featured 12 instruments – including pipes, whistles, bells, horns, cymbals, *halil* flutes, the *kinnor* and *nevel* lyres and the *tof* frame-drum.

A great breach occurred when Rome destroyed the Second Temple in Jerusalem in 70CE. After that calamity, Jews shunned the use of instruments for sacred music as a sign of mourning. This ban was soon lifted outside places of worship. Wedding parties stimulated religious melodies and secular festivities wherever Jews settled.

Below *Broadway pioneers George and Ira Gershwin were influenced by Yiddish theatre and popular Jewish music.*

RAM'S HORN

The exception to the ban on synagogue instruments is the *shofar*, the ram's horn, which is blown on Rosh Hashanah, the Jewish New Year. The *shofar* is meant to awaken people from their spiritual slumber and call them to repentance. One name for Rosh Hashanah is Yom Teru'ah, or the 'day of blowing'. The instrument is arguably the oldest known to mankind.

CHANTING AND MELODY

Other than the *shofar* and organs at weddings, all Orthodox synagogue music is sung. One sage called singing 'the fruit of the mouth'. The oldest modes are reserved for chanting weekly portions of the Torah and Prophets, and special markings written above and below the holy words, called *te'amim*, denote their tune.

Early medieval synagogues allowed more tuneful leeway with hymns and *piyuttot*, or liturgical poetry. These were and still are sung to a particular *nusah*, or melody pattern, akin to the Arabic *maqam*, Indian raga, Byzantine hymnody or Roman plainsong. The *nusah* denotes special times, so that someone with a discerning ear can enter a synagogue blindfolded and immediately tell from hearing everyday prayers, like the *amidah*, whether it is the Sabbath, a high holy day, morning service or evening service.

CANTORS AND CHOIRS

Over time the virtuoso *hazzan* (cantor) began to displace the more humdrum *shaliach tzibbur*, or prayer leader, and his role increased as congregants' knowledge of Hebrew diminished. The period between the two world wars is known as the 'golden age of *hazzanut*'.

Above *Frank London and his Klezmatics use jazz to breathe life into old European Jewish* klezmer.

The synagogue choir, originally an *ad hoc* body of harmonic responders, grew in stature and opulence with exposure to Western classical music. In 1882 the Polish-born Jewish composer Louis Lewandowski scored an entire choral service, *Todah ve-Zimrah*, or 'Thanks and Song', for Berlin's Oranienburgerstrasse Temple.

KLEZMER

From the 16th century, eastern European *Klezmorim*, or 'wandering folk musicians', and the *badchen* (jester or compère), were staple fare at weddings. Like their Sephardi counterparts, Ashkenazim absorbed local tunes and techniques into their repertoires. Players employed plaintive or ecstatic ornamentation and also mimicked the synagogue *hazzan* or fervent Hassidic *nigun* (often wordless improvizations). The resultant mixture gives *klezmer* its distinctive 'Jewish feel' to this day.

Since the 1970s klezmer and ladino have revived as Diaspora Jews rediscovered their roots. Some adherents favour hybrids with rock, folk and jazz, such as the American group, Klezmatics. Interestingly, some of the most skilful klezmer practitioners are non-Jewish Germans, like Tickle in the Heart, or Poles, like Kroke.

Above *Gustav Mahler, perhaps the greatest composer of Jewish origin, in the loggia of Vienna Opera House, 1907.*

CLASSICAL COMPOSERS

Medieval Arab theorists inspired Jews to study music as a science, and in time certain Italian and Provençal Jews embraced secular music composition.

The 19th-century enlightenment led to an explosion of Jewish talent in Germany and France, with composers like Felix and Fanny Mendelssohn, Claude Offenbach, Fromental Halévy, Giacomo Meyerbeer and Gustav Mahler. Many became Christians, thus casting doubt on their definition as 'Jewish composers'. Even so, hints of *klezmer* and synagogue melody appear in the majestic orchestrations of the newly Catholic Mahler.

Arnold Schoenberg shocked audiences with atonal experimentations, and inspired numerous imitators after fleeing Austria for America in 1934. More conventional were the American Jewish composers Aaron Copland and Leonard Bernstein. Both evoked a specifically American classical oeuvre, as in Copland's *Appalachian Spring* and Bernstein's *West Side Story*. In more contemplative works such as *Chichester Psalms* and his Third Symphony *Kaddish*, Bernstein set Hebrew texts to modern music.

Jews including Philip Glass and Steve Reich pioneered minimalism and experimentation with electronics in the 1960s. Both addressed Jewish themes – Glass in his *Einstein on the Beach* and Reich in *Tehillim* (Psalms), *Proverb*, *The Cave* (about Abraham and Hebron) and *Different Trains*, which evokes trucks en route to Auschwitz.

Jews have excelled as virtuoso performers, including pianists Arthur Rubinstein and Vladimir Ashkenazy.

JEWS AND JAZZ

From the early 1900s, black American and Jewish musicians practised and performed together in large cities like Chicago and New York. Several Yiddish tunes were reinterpreted as Jazz numbers, including *Burton on the Ritz*, derived from *Bei Mir Bist Du Shein*. Al Jolson moved from traditional Jewish music to become a leading Jazz, blues and ragtime singer.

Others who followed Jolson's Tin Pan Alley path included the songwriter Irving Berlin and Brazilian jazz diva, Flora Purim. George Gershwin bridged the chasm between 'high classical' music and Jazz with such rousing works as *Rhapsody in Blue*. The great swing clarinettist Benny Goodman was born in Chicago to Jewish immigrants and broke down racial segregation in America by working with black musicians.

Below *Stan Getz (1927–91), the American saxophonist who blended Brazilian bossa nova with jazz.*

Above *Arthur Rubinstein, classical pianist, received international acclaim for his interpretation of Chopin.*

ROCK AND ROLL

It is hard to imagine modern rock music without Jewish songwriters Jerry Leiber and Mike Stoller who helped launch the genre. Phil Spector pioneered the 1960s 'wall of sound' technique. In Britain, Brian Epstein managed the Beatles. Notable performers include Gene Simmons of Kiss, Marc Bolan of T Rex, Beastie Boys, Bob Dylan, Leonard Cohen, Ramones, Simon and Garfunkel, Paula Abdul, and converts to Judaism Sammy Davis Jr and Ike Turner.

THE SOUNDS OF ISRAEL

The sensitive songwriter Naomi Shemer drew heavily on the French chanson tradition of the 1960s, before releasing her song *Yerushalayim Shel Zahav* (Jerusalem of Gold) just before the Six Day War. It became in effect a second national anthem.

By the 1980s the singers Ofra Haza, Zehava Ben and the band Ethnix blended East and West to great effect. Hybrid forms and originality now typify Israeli music, examples of which include Yehuda Poliker, of Greek Jewish origin, who shifts from playing bazouki to hard electric rock, and Ahinoam Nini, who mixes jazz, 'indie' folk and Yemenite sounds.

Jewish Philosophers and Politicians

Even in rejecting aspects of traditional Judaism, thinkers such as Freud and Derrida showed signs of engaging with Judaic concepts, thus revealing a shared Jewish identity.

Perhaps the most revolutionary Jewish thinker of the 20th century was Sigmund Freud (1856–1939), who created psychoanalysis and explored the human unconscious. Convinced that neurosis resulted from repressed impulses and sexual drives, Freud drew on medicine, myth and dreams to explain how the mind works. Freudian terms such as the ego, the pleasure principle, paranoia, guilt feelings, subconscious, peer pressure and regression are repeatedly used and misused in everyday English conversation.

PSYCHOLOGY AND THEORY

Sigmund Freud was not a practising Jew and his books *Totem and Taboo* and *The Future of an Illusion* spoke of religion as the antithesis of reason and experience. None the less he accepted that faith was part of the human psyche. All his psychologist colleagues bar Karl Jung were Jewish. Sigmund's daughter, Anna, became a pioneer in child psychology.

Freud influenced other thinkers, including Jews such as Franz Boas (1858–1942) and Claude Lévi-Strauss (1908–2009) the founder of structural anthropology. While Lévi-Strauss analysed 'primitive' societies, Raymond Aron (1905–83) and Walter Benjamin (1892–1940) cast their gaze at modern civilization. The Parisian-born Aron asked how ordinary people made sense of industrial progress and political competition.

***Below** Hailed as the father of modern anthropology, Franz Boas studied people in their physical environment.*

SOCIOLOGISTS

Walter Benjamin killed himself while trying to escape Nazis on the Franco-Spanish border. Even more than Freud, this translator, essayist and philosopher wrestled with his Jewish identity. He individualistically applied the ideas of Goethe, Marx, Brecht and Jewish mysticism to current literature and aesthetics, and his prescient posthumous works *Illuminations* and *Arcades* considered the shopping mall and street life as epitomizing contemporary society. One of his last books, *Theses on the Philosophy of History*, addressed the Jewish quest for a messiah and humanity's clash with nihilism.

Another Jewish-origin pioneer of the link between words and ideas was the Austrian-born Cambridge philosopher and former 'logical positivist', Ludwig Wittgenstein. He and other Jewish thinkers such as Benjamin, Levi-Strauss and Theodor Adorno laid the basis for a post-war school called structuralism. Its most celebrated figure was Jacques Derrida (1930–2007). Derrida pioneered 'deconstruction', a method of minutely interrogating texts for signs of true meaning obscured by written convention, which has been profoundly influential.

***Above** Hermann Cohen. German neo-Kantian philosophers wrestled with Jewish topics in his many books.*

***Below** 'Philosophers have interpreted the world; the point, however, is to change it' – Karl Marx, 1875.*

PIONEERS IN ECONOMICS

New thinking in economics, jokingly called 'the dismal science', also owes much to Jews. Born into an English Sephardi family in 1772, David Ricardo became one of the most influential political economists. Monetarist Milton Friedman inspired Thatcherism in 1970s Britain and President Reagan's supply-side economics in America. Academic development economist Jeffrey Sachs draws on Jewish philosophy, not least Maimonides' theory of facilitating self-help as the highest form of charity. He has advised many Latin American and post-communist states.

Finally, George Soros of Hungary has turned his billions gained in speculation to promoting 'open societies' worldwide. Soros' ideas come from Jewish philosopher Karl Popper, who championed transparency as the ultimate tool against authoritarian systems.

Interestingly, many Jews in the Marxist camp veered from narrower economic analysis to investigating social change.

NEW THINKING IN JUDAISM

Thousands of believing 19th-century Jews sought a middle path, one that married Jewish heritage with modern realities. Exposure to Western academic methods led to radical new outlooks. From the 1950s onwards French philosopher Emmanuel Levinas (1906–95) popularized Talmudic methods to a new generation of secular scholars. More mainstream Orthodox Jews responded to the Haskalah spirit and Hassidic fervour by promoting the Mussar movement of contemplation and ethical introspection started by Rav Israel Salanter (1810–83). Salanter was inspired by the writings of Moshe Chaim Luzzatto (1707–46, an Italian kabbalist and rabbi.

Left *Claude Lévi-Strauss, pioneer of structuralism, at the opening of the Musee du Quai Branly, Paris, 2006.*

THE NON-JEWISH JEW AND DIASPORA POLITICIANS

And yet the question remains, is there anything specifically Jewish about thinkers on general matters who just happen to be Jewish? To Isaac Deutscher (1907–67), the Polish-born British historian, Marxist activist and biographer of Stalin and Trotsky, it was possible, indeed almost inevitable, to be a 'non-Jewish Jew'. Though an atheist and foe of Jewish nationalism, he felt himself a 'Jew by force of my unconditional solidarity with the persecuted, because I feel the pulse of Jewish history.'

Above *Seasoned diplomat and former US Secretary of State Henry Kissinger (right) conversing with Russian President Vladimir Putin in 2004.*

Germany's Chancellor from 1909 to 1917 was Theobald von Bethmann Hollweg, a descendant of a prominent Frankfurt Jewish banking family; while in Italy two Jews, Sydney Sonnino and Luigi Luzzatti, became prime ministers in 1909–10 and 1910–11 respectively. France has had five Jewish-origin prime ministers in the last century, most notably Leon Blum before World War II and Pierre Mendes-France after, both from the left. For 12 years Bruno Kreisky was Austria's Chancellor, and Henry Kissinger, who arrived in America in 1938 as a refugee from Nazi Germany, rose to become possibly Washington's most influential Secretary of State during 1973–77. Perhaps most powerful of all was Benjamin Disraeli, the first and only British Prime Minister of Jewish origin in 1868 and 1874–80; he spoke proudly of his people's heritage, though he was converted to Anglicanism aged 13.

Index

PICTURE ACKNOWLEDGEMENTS

akg–images: 15t, 19b, 19t, 23t, 35t, 37b, 38b, 40b, 40t, 42b, 42t, 46t, 47t, 66t, 70t, 71t, 73b, 116t; /Bible Land Pictures/www.Bi 28b; /Bildarchiv Pisarek 21b, 41t, 57b, 69b, 124t; /Erich Lessing 22t, 32t, 58t, 63bl, 67t; /Heiner Heine 14b; /IAM/WorldHistory Archive 27b; /Israel Images 17t, 30b, 82b, 90t; /Suzanne Heid 31b; /ullstein bild 61, 72t.
Alamy: /© 19th era 2 27t; /© AF archive 117b; /© Art Directors & TRIP 23b, 51b; /© Art of Travel 16b; /© Bernie Epstein 114b; /© David Hoffman 102b; /© Eddie Gerald 109b; /© Hanan Isachar 83t; /© Idealink Photography 35b; /© Interfoto 80t; /© Israel Images 88b, 90bl, 91; /© Israel Imagesi 108b; /© Ivan Vdovin 28t; /© Janice Hazeldine 101b; /© Laura S Goodman 54b; /© Lebrecht Music and Arts Photo Library 55t; /© Nathan Benn 39t, 85t; /© North Wind Picture Archives 45, 46b; /© Paris Marais 103b; /© Peter Titmuss 54t; /© PhotoStock-Israel 82t; /© Pictorial Press Ltd 121t; /© Robert Fried 106t; /© Sally and Richard Greenhill 111bl; /© Shaun Higson colour 26b; /© Steve Allen Travel Photography 78; /© vario images GmbH & Co. KG 39b; /© White House Photo 92b; /© Yurij Brykaylo 26t; /©RIA Novosti 125t; /Art Directors & TRIP 103t; /Israel Images 96t.
The Art Archive: 71b, 122b; /Culver Pictures 64b, 112b; /Domenica del Corriere/Collection Dagli Orti 48t; /Fondation Thiers Paris/ Gianni Dagli Orti 25; /Gianni Dagli Orti 50b; /Karl Marx Museum Trier/Alfredo Dagli Orti 124br; /Musée Départemental des Vosges Epinal/Gianni Dagli Orti 15br; /Musée des 2 Guerres Mondiales Paris/Gianni Dagli Orti 65b; /Musée du Louvre Paris/Collection Dagli Orti 33t; /Museum of London 63t; /National Archives Washington DC 52b, 74b; /National Palace Mexico City/Gianni Dagli Orti 13t; /Nationalmuseet Copenhagen Denmark/Collection Dagli Orti 14t; /Navy Historical Service Vincennes France/Gianni Dagli Orti 18b; /Nicholas J. Saunders 63br; /Palazzo Pitti Florence/Collection Dagli Orti 11t; /Private Collection/Marc Charmet 31t, 64t, 76b; /Rijksmuseum Amsterdam/Superstock 22b; /Russian Historical Museum Moscow/Collection Dagli Orti 34t; /Stephanie Colasanti 9, 10b, 107b; /Szapiro Collection Paris/Gianni Dagli Orti 10t; /Tate Gallery London/Eileen Tweedy 30t; /Topkapi Museum Istanbul/ Gianni Dagli Orti 16t, 18t; /University Library Istanbul/Gianni Dagli Orti 24.
Bridgeman Images: 12b, 13bl, 20b, 43b, 50t, 92t, 107t, 115t; /© Edifice 43t; /© SZ Photo 13br, 70b; /© Zev Radovan 110t; /Archives Charmet 20t, 51t; /Gift of James A. de Rothschild, London 116b; /Giraudon 8, 37t; /Peter Willi 56b; /Photo © Christie's Images 44; /Photo © Philip Mould Ltd, London 57t; /Seth G. Sweetser Fund 36t; /The Steiglitz Collection and donated with contribition from Erica & Ludwig Jesselson 34b.
Cody Images: 7b, 68b, 72b, 75b, 86b.
Corbis: 48b, 86t, 111tl, 111tr, 113t; /© Adrian Andrusier/Lebrecht Music & Arts 41, 49; /© Andy Aitchison/In Pictures 98b; /© Ann Johansson 104b; /© Atlantide Phototravel 108t; /© Bettmann 53t, 53b, 58b, 65t, 66b, 67b, 75t, 81b, 83b, 87t, 89b, 96b, 98t, 100t, 112t, 117t, 118t, 118bl, 124bl; /© Bojan Brecelj 122t; /© Cezaro de Luca/epa 106b; /© Christel Gerstenberg 12t; /© Colin McPherson 119tr; /© David James/Sygma 121b; /© David Rubinger 89t; /© David Sutherland 5, 74t; /© Ed Kashi 84t; /© epa 73t; /© Eyal Warshavsky/Corbis 99b; /© Gianni Giansanti/Sygma 77t; /© Hanan Isachar 29t; /© Hulton-Deutsch Collection 47b, 68t, 84b, 87b, 88t, 97, 115b; /© Ira Wyman/Sygma 119b; /© Katarina Stoltz/Reuters 60; /© Kevin Fleming 101t; /© Lebrecht Arts & Music 104t, 123tl; /© Lee Snider/Photo Images 6b, 36b; /© Li Erben 123tr; /© Marc Garanger 105b; /© Marcus Fhrer/epa 69t; / © Melvyn Longhurst 55b; /© Michael Freeman 85b;/© Michael Nicholson 62t; /© Michel Selboun/Sygma 32b, 33b; /© Nathan Benn 2, 109t; /© Nathan Benn/Ottochrome 105t; /© Pascal Parrot/Sygma 111br; /© Peter M. Wilson 41b; /© Pimentel Jean/Corbis KIPA 7t; / © Reuters 100b; /© Richard T. Nowitz 29b; /© Robert Holmes 11b; / © Sophie Bassouls/Sygma 118br; /© Stapleton Collection 59; /© Swim Ink 2, LLC 80b; /© Ted Spiegel 3, 95; /© Walter Mcbride 119tl.
Rex Features: 123b; /Alinari 56t, 94; /Assaf Shillo 99t; /Chameleons Eye 93; /Courtesy Everett Collection 102t; /Everett Collection 77b, 120b, 120t; /Israel Sun 79; /Marco Marianella 113b; /Roman Koszowski 76t; /SIPA PRESS 81t, 114t, 125b.